DATE DUE

REFERENDUM FOR ISOLATION

UNIVERSITY OF GEORGIA MONOGRAPHS, NO. 6

Referendum
for
Isolation

Defeat of Article Ten of the
League of Nations Covenant

By

JOHN CHALMERS VINSON

DEPARTMENT OF HISTORY
UNIVERSITY OF GEORGIA

UNIVERSITY OF GEORGIA PRESS
ATHENS   1961

To my parents

NAN WHARTON AND THOMAS CHALMERS

VINSON

Contents

Preface

THE defeat of the League of Nations has been described often as a blow from which American foreign policy did not recover before a new catastrophe overtook it. Personal hatred, partisan spite, and blind stubbornness have been emphasized as prime causes for rejection of the League in the United States. With these views I have no quarrel. However, intrigued by the theory that even the most partisan claim must, to be effective, rest in some measure on an element of truth, I have sought to isolate the element of truth in the League debate, to examine the logical as opposed to the emotional causes for its rejection. Basic differences of opinion as to the wisest course for American foreign policy were most sharply drawn in the debates on Article Ten of the Covenant. Woodrow Wilson unyieldingly maintained through Article Ten that the preservation of peace required of League members a guarantee to protect by force if necessary the political and territorial integrity of the signatory powers. His opponents, from the irreconcilables to the mild reservationists, favored altering Article Ten so as to eliminate a binding commitment to preserve the peace by coercion. A study of Article Ten leads to the conclusion that the opposing positions could not be reconciled and that on honest difference of opinion rested the effectiveness of much of the highly distorted and bitterly partisan argument that helped to defeat the League. As this one topic has been of greatest interest to me, I have made no attempt to present all facets of the League debate or make any final judgment as to the ultimate significance of the debate over Article Ten in the defeat of the League. Rather it has been my purpose to suggest to those already familiar with the League debate a vital and, it seems to me, somewhat neglected phase of that momentous struggle.

In the preparation of this work I am indebted to the Social Science Research Council for allowing me to participate in a summer research seminar in 1956. From this experience grew the interest that prompted my study of Article Ten. I am also indebted to the John Simon Guggenheim Foundation for a fellowship that allowed me the time for research and writing on this and other projects. I am grateful for a grant from the General Research Fund of the University of Georgia, making possible the publication of this work.

I have been greatly aided in the preparation of this book by many members of the staff of the Library of Congress. Professor George Osborn of the University of Florida assisted me by reading my manuscript and making helpful suggestions. Ralph Stephens, Director of the University of Georgia Press, and his staff have worked long and patiently in my behalf.

Finally I must thank Almira, Chal, and Douglas for putting up with me during the difficult days while the "black book" was in preparation.

                                                          J. Chal Vinson

History Department
University of Georgia

CHAPTER I

Traditions Versus Article Ten

WHEN the United States Senate and the American people rejected Woodrow Wilson's version of the League of Nations in 1920, they made a decision comparable in significance to any in their history. The debate was the climax, during the nation's first forty years as a great power, in the struggle to alter the appropriate traditions of the nineteenth century, nationalism and isolationism, to the demands of the country's radically new position of power in the twentieth century.

Destiny posed in 1920 three questions: Would the United States accept the responsibility for world leadership, promote peace through a system of collective security, and use military as well as moral force to achieve these ends? The last question was the most important for it was the test of sincerity in discharging the other two. The negative answer given in 1920 to all three questions was not foisted upon a powerless people by unscrupulous parliamentarians in the Senate. The answer was consistent with American experience and tradition in foreign affairs. It was representative of the will of the majority of the people and of their informed leadership.

The League of Nations, in general outline, represented a logical extension of an American ideal, a world organization to promote peace. In this respect it won the endorsement of the majority of Americans. But in practice its specific method for achieving its noble aim, the binding commitment to use force to quell aggression implied in Article Ten, was in complete contradiction to American traditions in foreign affairs. The Article provided that "the members of the League undertake to respect and preserve as against external aggression the territorial integrity and

1

existing political independence of all Members of the League. In case of any such aggression, the Executive Council shall advise upon the means by which this obligation shall be fulfilled."[1] Woodrow Wilson was not engaging in platform oratory when he called Article Ten "the heart of the Covenant." At the same time it was a bold departure from two of the nation's most honored traditions, non-entanglement and non-militarism. The nation since its birth had eschewed any permanent commitment with other nations. Equally important, America, unlike the nations of Europe, had no large standing army and refused, even in its unilateral actions, to recognize military force as an instrument of foreign policy.

As with all legal documents, there were many differing interpretations as to the precise intent of Article Ten. Yet, there was substantial agreement from all sources on two vital points: it was a pledge which the United States was morally bound to discharge; the consultation provided in the Article must result in positive action if the League was to function. The debate ranged around three questions: Was it necessary for American agreement to accept such a pledge? How frequently would action be demanded? How extensive must be the use of force?

Woodrow Wilson, the chief protagonist for Article Ten, emphasized that it was the destiny and duty of the United States to accept the pledge. The moral pledge to use force must always be honored when the necessity arose. At the same time, he assured the nation such crises would be extremely rare if they occurred at all. The unified determination of the nations to punish outlaws would stifle aggression before it developed. This was a league for peace, not war.

Opponents of Article Ten described it as unnecessary either for American security or for an effective league. They warned that its moral pledge bound America to repress foreign quarrels all over the world. To meet its obligation America must become an armed camp, unceasingly providing troops to be deployed by the superstate in Geneva. They, of course, exaggerated the obligations undertaken, just as Wilson and the friends of the League underestimated the commitments.

Almost no senators, Republican or Democratic, accepted Article Ten on its merits. Most Republican leaders opposed it. Few of Wilson's advisors accepted its principle and almost none of them thought it politically expedient to demand its adoption without reservation. Nevertheless, Wilson saw Article Ten without reservation as the dividing line between an effective and an oratorical league. Time and again as a crisis was reached in the long debate on the League, Article Ten proved to be the irreconcilable point of disagreement between the President and the Senate. Unwillingness to alter the traditional policy, unilateral and non-military, was thus a powerful, probably decisive, reason for the American decision to reject the League. Even those states that did join the League found it difficult to honor the commitments that ran counter to the inertia of human nature and the force of the living past. Thus the question was not simply adopting a league—there was no magic in a title. The question resolved itself, as Wilson and Henry Cabot Lodge, the chief protagonists of the opposing forces, declared so many times, to the issue of accepting the full obligations of Article Ten or so amending those obligations as virtually to nullify its provisions.

Hence, while some evil partisans in the Senate did plot the defeat of the League for the meanest of reasons and an ill and at times unreasonable President blindly rejected compromise, larger and more significant forces were at work against it. A partisan issue usually has a basis in popular belief and, indeed, is effective only to the degree that this is true. It was fatal to a League incorporating Article Ten that the American people were unwilling, in the absence of any recognized clear and present danger, to purchase the security they did not seem to need at the cost of traditions cherished for generations.

Time and again for two decades after the League's defeat, popular unwillingness to accept responsibility and obligation was translated by American statesmen into peace plans free of guarantees and unsupported by military sanctions. There was the abortive Harding association of nations, the Washington Conference for the Limitation of Naval Armament, and the Kellogg-Briand Pact, all partaking of a measure of cooperation but denying Article Ten's com-

pulsive commitment. Not until a second war engulfed the
nation did the theme of power for peace become respectable
again.

Insofar as real issues as opposed to specious partisan
pretensions determined the outcome of a debate more
marked by emotional frenzy than logical analysis, the
disagreement over Article Ten was responsible for the defeat of the League of Nations in the United States.

But in the everyday affairs of a nation the academic
luxury of separating true and false issues is largely impossible
and meaningless. Article Ten, a fundamental issue in debate,
was also one of the most prolific sources of the personal,
partisan bitterness that overshadowed the Senate debate
on the League. Wilson, the man and the Democrat, was the
center of this phase of the debate and Article Ten was his
personal creation. To him it was the indivisible essence of
the Covenant. Only because of his unyielding devotion to
the ideal it embodied was it included in the Covenant at all.
Both for its merits as a radically new approach to American
policy and its personal implications as the personal contribution of the President, Article Ten inevitably became
the focal point of attack on the League by both partisan
and patriot.

The opposition manifest to Article Ten on its merits
had origins older than the nation itself—the ideals of isolation and non-militarism. Both ideals were revered as basic
supports of the great national ideal of republican government. Political entanglements with autocratic powers were
shunned as leading inevitably to the destruction of democracy. America must be isolated to develop as a free republic. In turn, this necessity for isolation was strengthened
by the economic theory that America's concern with Europe
was commerce, "not politics or war."[2] In accord with this
ideal, American commerce with all parts of the world expanded while its international commitments remained static.
Even at the end of the nineteenth century when commerce
demanded imperialism many leaders warned that territorial
expansion endangered the American system of government.
Imperialism was "at war with the best traditions, principles,
and interests of the American people."[3] It would lead the
United States into European systems of power politics

opposed to all traditional American ideals of government. Isolation, it was argued, guaranteed the spiritual as well as the material security of the United States. To engage in direct political contact with other governments, to accept international obligations limiting American freedom of action in foreign affairs would corrupt and kill American democracy. The United States had a duty to the world, an obligation to keep itself apart, to perfect a model government, and to serve as an example to regenerate the outworn political systems of Europe.

Non-militarism, to a large degree a beneficial result of isolation, was equally sanctioned by tradition. The geographical remoteness of America provided security from attack and made a non-military state possible. The democratic theory abjured physical force and declared its faith in man's essential goodness and ultimate perfectibility. There was every reason to curb the military, which constituted a threat to the very existence of democracy and a constant invitation for the ambitious to seize the sword and march to dictatorship. The logic of these arguments was undergirded by the lessons of experience. The peaceful democracy prospered; the soldier was little needed. No military tradition developed. The individual American had an antipathy for the professional military career with its iron discipline, set caste system, and limited economic rewards. As a business man he resented the taxes to support the military and denounced its waste of resources.

Isolation and non-militarism in nineteenth-century America were infrequently disturbed by international crisis. Unlike European states America did not have to develop diplomacy to maintain national security against ceaseless pressure. Diplomacy was employed only spasmodically and its occasional use achieved apparently unqualified success. The relation of diplomacy to military force as correlative means for achieving national objectives did not impress itself on Americans in the hard school of experience. When they combined force and diplomacy, as they did in innumerable instances, they did so unconsciously. They did not allow the unpleasant fact of participation in nine European wars and thirty-seven Indian wars in 180 years to contradict the worthy theory of American non-militarism. The aberrations from the theory were so numerous as to cause one critic to comment that if the expansion of the United States resulted from "humanitarian and pacific traditions, never in the history of the world has virtue been more bountifully rewarded."[4] The American people entered the twentieth century traditionally unaware of any connection between power and politics, firmly convinced of their unfailing devotion to peace-loving humanitarianism. Their experience and attitude left Americans uninformed as to the nature of diplomacy and made it difficult for them to accept the unaccustomed obligations of a League of Nations.

Running counter to tradition, it would seem at first glance, was the growth, in this same century, of organized peace societies. From their plans for promoting world peace through international organization might have grown the seeds of a future league. But on examination the subservience of these societies to the traditions of isolation and non-militarism and their distaste for diplomacy become apparent. They were based on the democratic ideal of law enforced by moral suasion and public opinion. Whatever their virtues, they were not prototypes for the League of Nations. The oldest of these, the American Peace Society, rejected any recourse to military force. As William Ladd, one of its important spokesmen, said: "Physical power to enforce the laws of our Congress, or the decrees of our Court, forms no part of our plan." Compliance with court decisions would be compelled through the power of public opinion, a force which no civilized nation could withstand —a factor many times stronger than a police force in domestic society. Ladd, as did many critics of the League decades later, opposed the use of military sanctions as being war within itself. All efforts to enforce peace by military might in the past had been fruitless and would continue to be in the future. Moral force alone could bring peace.[5] Throughout the nineteenth century moral sanctions remained the reliance of all the American societies and continued to be the rule well into the twentieth century.

Such were the traditions of the nineteenth century, hallowed by unbroken success. These traditions continued to dominate thought even though America's rapid industrial growth and rise to world power in the Spanish-American war brought new conditions. There began to be challenges to the old standards of foreign policy, but the traditional assumptions were not seriously undermined. In vain did Theodore Roosevelt, as Assistant Secretary of the Navy, speaking to the War College in 1897, voice a new ideal of diplomacy for a new age. Diplomacy, he declared, was "utterly useless" without "force behind it." The diplomatist was the "servant, not the master, of the soldier."[6]

With the turn of the century a new group of peace societies began to grow and to reflect the ideal of reliance on physical force to maintain international order. One example was the Universal Peace Congress, including American delegates, meeting in Monaco in 1902, which drew up a Treaty of Pacigerant Alliance. All disputes were subject to arbitration; the member states were "constrained to keep faith." The constraint, not clearly defined, appeared to rest on the willingness of member states to aid arbitrators "with the means of enforcing their award."[7] The North Carolina Peace Society, another of the new organizations, in April, 1908, called on Roosevelt at the White House suggesting to him that "effective arbitration necessitates treaties between our country and all other governments, by which the contracting powers mutually agree to respect each other's territory and sovereignty in said territory and to arbitrate all other questions of law and fact."[8] The organization, with Roosevelt's blessing, took steps in 1910 to promote its theories through a nation-wide organization—the American Peace and Arbitration League. This approach to peace was sponsored also by the National Peace Congress, which was organized in 1908. In 1911 at its third national meeting, the National Peace Congress endorsed the resolution of editor Hamilton Holt of the *Independent* proposing a League for Peace based on arbitration and rejecting the "use of force for any purpose whatsoever." At the same meeting a resolution by Congressman James Slayden was adopted proposing that the status quo of all Latin-American republics be mutually guaranteed by a general American treaty.[9]

In Congress the most outspoken champion of peace, Richard Bartholdt, proposed in 1904 a plan for compulsory arbitration. He presented it in expanded form the next year to the Thirteenth Interparliamentary Conference at Brussels. Bartholdt hoped the legislative bodies in all the major nations would sponsor compulsory arbitration. In a statement foreshadowing the idea later incorporated in Article Ten, he required all members of his proposed organization to guarantee a respect for the territory and sovereignty of other members. Other proposals allowed each nation to arm itself as it saw fit and to withdraw from the organization at any time. War was recognized as a lawful method of settling disputes. Last was a provision that the armed forces of all the nations "be at the service of the Congress for the enforcement of any decrees rendered by the Hague Court according to treaties of arbitration."[10]

A radically different approach, recognizing the relationship of diplomacy and power and calling for the maintenance of peace through military preparedness, was advocated in Congress during these years by Richmond P. Hobson. The naval hero of the Spanish-American War sought for America a navy large enough to establish "an equilibrium in two oceans." Armament and peace were linked in "an intimate and inseparable relation . . . as correlative means for justice."[11] Hobson's proposal to require the building of six new dreadnaughts in 1908 tended to obscure his role as a peacemaker in the minds of most of his colleagues, even though he suggested setting aside one per cent of the cost of each battleship to promote the cause of peace.[12]

In practice, aside from theory, naval appropriations during these years, with the energetic support of Theodore Roosevelt as President, were the largest ever made by Congress in peacetime. The House, attempting to halt this trend after Roosevelt left office, in 1910 adopted a resolution in accord with the petitions of citizens and peace societies, requesting the President to set up a five-man commission to consider the possibilities of using existing international agencies to limit armament. If nations could be made to feel secure, they would be willing to disarm. Security might be achieved by combining "the navies of the world into an international force for the preservation of universal peace. . . ."[13] While President William Howard Taft did not implement the resolutions, interest in disarmament continued in Congress. However, it is significant to note, the "international force" suggested in 1910 was not included in the next resolution for disarmament adopted in 1913.[14]

The trend in Congress away from military sanctions was sharply reversed for a time after the outbreak of the First World War. Many resolutions for peace were presented in Congress in 1915, a high percentage of them including provision for police action by an international army and navy.[15] None of these resolutions passed in 1915, but one was adopted in August, 1916, in the form of an amendment to the naval appropriations bill. It provided for the termination of America's naval building program if a conference of powers at the end of the war agreed to disarm and establish an effective international organization. Provision for an international police force, made in earlier drafts, was deleted in the final version adopted by Congress.[16] Not for many years did Congress again support the idea of an international police force. Thus Congress from 1900 to 1920 was moving toward disarmament but away from a coercive military league of nations.

More vital than its opinions on any specific plan for peace was the Senate's general position on control of foreign policy in the two decades before the League debate. Determined to protect and expand its prerogatives, the Senate emasculated or rejected every general arbitration treaty presented to it during these two decades. Senators charged that the Presidents sought through arbitration treaties to make the Executive Department independent of all other departments. It was the duty of the Senate to halt so dangerous a tendency by protecting its rights and at the same time the rights of the people. They followed this course with such zeal that they were accused of seeking "to make the Secretary of State a mere clerk of the Senate Committee on Foreign Relations."[17] Whatever the merits of these arguments, it is significant that the long-standing struggle for power was raging unabated in the second decade of the twentieth century.

It was no idle debate; it had far-reaching implications for

American foreign policy. In 1897 and again in 1911 the Senate safeguarded its rights in general arbitration treaties with Great Britain by reservations so drastic as to kill the treaties. On both of these occasions public opinion was manifestly in favor of the treaties. But the Senate's success in the struggle with the Executive was more clearly shown in the arbitration treaties that were adopted than in those that failed. Even so powerful a President as Theodore Roosevelt could not win adoption of arbitration treaties in 1905 without bowing to the Senate's will by accepting reservations that he declared rendered the treaties a "sham" and a "step backward."[18] No President during these two decades overcame or successfully compromised with the Senate's ardent opposition to any international peace program reducing its prerogatives.

In addition to the Senate's determination to maintain a voice in treaty making, two other tendencies weighed against acceptance of any revolutionary change in foreign policy. In the first place, any disagreement on domestic policy (and there were many in Wilson's day) the Senate carried into its appraisals of a President's foreign policy. In the second place, the Senate was conservative by design and by inclination; there was nothing in the recent history of the body to encourage Wilson when he began to advocate a revolution in American foreign policy. Knowing the Senate's history well he was never optimistic about his chances of converting ingrained opposition to support.

Outside of Congress well-intentioned leaders such as Andrew Carnegie or Edward Ginn sought to promote peace. More significant because of his political importance were the ideals of peace championed by Theodore Roosevelt, both as President and private citizen. As early as 1905, he advocated that the nations, with the active aid of the United States, take steps "toward creating something like an organization of the civilized nations" invested with authority to curb offending nations.[19] Three years later he told a delegation from the North Carolina Peace Society that "effective arbitration necessitates agreements between all the powers to respect each others' territory and sovereignty in said territory, and to arbitrate all other questions."[20] He returned to this theme, after yielding to the Senate reserva-

tionist on arbitration treaties, in his Nobel Prize speech in
1910, declaring that the nations must undertake seriously the
task "of devising some method" to render effective the
decisions of arbitral courts. The "method," he suggested,
must rest on force, real or potential, sufficient to compel
compliance. To this end he proposed a "combination between those great nations which sincerely desire peace,"
a solemn engagement to keep the peace themselves and
"prevent, by force if necessary, its being broken by others."
These were brave words, but Roosevelt did not always
live up to his words; it is apparent that he looked upon his
League for Peace as a distant goal, not an immediate possibility.[21]

Roosevelt in his alternately ardent and apathetic pattern
devoted little time to this project during the next four
years. The outbreak of the First World War focused his
attention once again on a league for peace and convinced
him that it must be the basis of postwar policy. To this end
he proposed in 1914 "A World League for the Peace of
Righteousness." Its main reliance was to be a binding agreement to "unitedly coerce the recalcitrant nation." The
collective armed power of civilization, Roosevelt declared,
must enforce civilization's determination "to do what is
right." These statements, issued just prior to the congressional elections of 1914, were intended to be used as a
means of criticizing the ultra-pacifist position of Wilson
and Bryan, the "cult of cowardice." Further, Roosevelt
sought to embarrass and undermine Wilson by showing
that the Democrats with no announced program for peace
had failed to look to the nation's postwar duty.[22]

Shortly after the election Roosevelt brought out a more
reasoned and less political program for peace. Here, as in
1910 at Christiania, he emphasized the need for the great
powers to agree in good faith to employ their combined
military forces to coerce any nation defying the decisions
of a world court. The United States, he added, must be one
of the "joint guarantors of world peace."[23]

A few weeks later Roosevelt published an even more
complete plan for a coercive peace association entitled
"Utopia or Hell." Guaranteeing territorial integrity, he
argued, was the only sound basis for assuring "the peace

of righteousness." In his plan for peace, he specified that a
league be formed consisting of two groups: the contracting
powers, civilized, well behaved, and willing to "use force
when force is required to back up righteousness," and the
"outside" powers, unwilling or unable "to guarantee to
help execute the decrees of the court by force" but allowed
to enjoy the benefits of the organization. The contracting
powers would "lay down the rule that the territorial integrity of each nation was inviolate; that it was to be
guaranteed absolutely its sovereign rights . . . in matters
affecting its honor and vital interest." All other matters
could be settled by an international court. The court would
be made effective by the determination of the nations
"to use their entire military force, if necessary, against any
nation which defied the decrees of the tribunal or which
violated any of the rights which in the rules it was ex-
pressly stipulated should be reserved to the several nations,
the rights to their territorial integrity and the like. . . ."

Throughout his disquisition Roosevelt emphasized that "this
treaty shall put force back of righteousness, shall provide
a method of securing by the exercise of force the observance
of solemn international obligations . . . by all the powers
covenanting to put their whole strength back of the fulfillment of the treaty obligations . . . by the willingness
and ability of great, free powers to put might back of right,
to make their protest against wrongdoing effective by, if
necessary, punishing the wrongdoer." Such an agreement,
he added, must not be entered into lightly but with the
determination "to redeem in the concrete promises we made
in the abstract" and to use force to accomplish this end if
necessary.[24] Here was the fundamental idea that Wilson was
to champion so strongly later on in Article Ten of the
League of Nations Covenant—the binding military guarantee
of territorial integrity. There was, however, one vital difference: Roosevelt's plan was in effect an alliance of the
great powers; Wilson's original plan was to end alliances
forever through a league of all nations. Nor is it clear
whether Roosevelt, in seeming to call for an immediate use
of force, defined his position accurately. It was still an ideal
toward which the nations should work rather than an immediate possibility. Privately he told a friend that an in-

ternational military agency in 1916 was as impractical as the ideal of universal suffrage was when the Magna Charta was signed. A year later he criticized the League to Enforce Peace for, among other faults, attempting a program for which the world was not yet ready.[25] Certainly Roosevelt's ideas were subject to change and never remotely approached a firm program, widely accepted.

Nevertheless, there was much similarity in the plans of the two leaders. Both recognized that force was necessary to establish order. Unfortunately partisan feeling was too keen for Roosevelt to see any good in Wilson's League or for Wilson to acknowledge Roosevelt's contribution until very late in the struggle. It was September 19, 1919, while on his last campaign, that Wilson endorsed Roosevelt's dictum that the powerful civilized nations "should combine by solemn agreement in a great world league for the peace of righteousness."

Not all advocates of peace were as willing as Roosevelt to live by the sword. Yet, there was much disillusionment with the strictly judicial theory of arbitration administered through a world court. That system, it was clear, had serious disadvantages. A court lacked authority to halt threatened conflicts at their source before they became dangerous. It could not compel states to use its facilities; it could not enforce decisions on recalcitrant nations. The theory of a political league able to meet these needs by virtue of the power and flexibility denied a judicial organization became increasingly popular as the widening catastrophy of world war mocked the peace societies' cherished ideal of order through law upheld by moral force. Conversely, the pacificist ideals of peace societies became increasingly suspect as the United States moved toward war.

A new peace organization was sorely needed. One was suggested by Hamilton Holt, who began writing articles in late 1914 renewing his proposal, made in 1911 to the National Peace Congress, for a league of peace capable of surmounting the defects inherent in the judicial approach to peace. Unlike Roosevelt, Holt still specifically recommended "total abstinence from the use of force" in his proposed league. Not all nations would join a league, he argued, and the threat of force would drive non-members into a counter-alliance.[26] Holt's ideas on the use of force rapidly altered in the last months of 1914 when he came to believe that force must be employed in achieving the essential aim of the peace movement—substituting law for war. Force, in fact, was almost wholly good when used in police action or in defense, even though it was evil when used aggressively. "The problem of the League of Peace," he declared with great insight, "is chiefly the problem of the use of force"—the balancing of controlled police action against ruthless aggression. By January he accepted Roosevelt's plan but wished to include disarmament in it. The use of American forces to maintain peace, Holt pointed out in a speech at Lake Mohonk early in 1915, was approved by many prominent leaders, including both ex-Presidents, Roosevelt and Taft.[27] A league must at least possess joint military strength sufficient to overcome the military threat of non-member states.

With the aid of Theodore Marburg and other members of the Century Association in New York City, Holt devoted much time early in 1915 to drafting a charter for an organization capable of turning idealism into action. The League of Peace, as it was first called, resulted.

The problem of the use of force was debated at great length in these organizational meetings; the decisions were most significant. The suggestion that recourse to force be optional was abandoned at the insistence of A. Lawrence Lowell, president of Harvard, who demanded automatic use of coercion against members failing to submit disputes to arbitration. This was the most extreme proposal the League was to adopt; although an even stronger proposal, a guarantee of territorial integrity and sovereignty of members against outside parties, almost the exact phrase later used in Article Ten, was adopted at the first of the planning sessions. This proposal was debated and finally deleted at the next meeting. The purpose of the League, it was agreed, should be to guarantee that no other member state should settle a dispute by other than amicable means under penalty of military coercion. But in the third of the preliminary meetings the word *guarantee* was dropped from this pledge; the use of force was limited strictly to compelling disputants to arbitrate. A specific guarantee of territorial and political integrity was debated for the third and last time at this meeting and rejected.[28] The League, it was made clear, would not assume responsibility for bringing about the final peaceful settlement of any dispute, although it was described as "A League of Nations, An Alliance of the Great Powers for the Enforcement of Peace."[29]

The League's purpose, as Theodore Marburg, chairman of these planning sessions, explained it, was to serve as "an international grand jury with power to hale the nation-law-breakers into court with a posse to bring it there if recalcitrant." It was not empowered to enforce the award made by the court. Such power, Marburg feared, might lead to oppression and injustice until such a time as the great majority of the nations became members.[30]

Despite its conservative endorsement of force the name of the organization was changed from the League of Peace to the League to Enforce Peace at the organizational meeting on the anniversary of the Battle of Bunker Hill, June 17, in Philadelphia. Those delegates who opposed any use of force brought forward an amendment to drop "enforce" from the title of the League and won by a voice vote. At that point, Lawrence Lowell declared, in an impassioned denunciation of the action: "Either we are here to *enforce* peace, or we are here for nothing at all!" He demanded a second vote on the amendment, this time by a show of hands. By a margin of eleven votes the delegates reversed their previous decision and decided to call the organization the League to Enforce Peace. The subsequent events at this meeting—the agreement to use military and economic sanction rather than providing a choice between the two—show that this victory, though narrow, gave complete control to those members who favored, although in a strictly limited way, the use of force to maintain peace.[31]

The organization adopted under the title "Warrant From History" an explanation of its ideals: "Throughout five thousand years of recorded history, peace, here and there established, has been kept, and its area has been widened, in one way only. Individuals have combined their efforts to suppress violence in the local community. . . . Always peace has been made and kept, when made and kept at all, by the superior power of superior numbers acting in unity for the common good.

"Mindful of this teaching of experience, we believe and solemnly urge that the time has come to devise and to create a working union of sovereign nations to establish peace among themselves and to guarantee it by all known and available sanctions at their command, to the end that civilization may be conserved, and the progress of mankind in comfort, enlightenment and happiness may continue."[32]

These aggressive statements of general purpose and the title, League to Enforce Peace, implied much stronger punitive powers than its leaders actually intended. Basically, the League reaffirmed the American tradition of the peaceful settlement of international disputes most recently exemplified in the unsuccessful Taft arbitration treaties. To those treaties the League simply appended a penalty clause. A title more representative of the organization's objective would have been the League to Enforce Consideration.[33] Its approach and methods, while frequently described as identical, actually were far removed from the ideas President Wilson was to advocate in the League of Nations.

Important in shaping the purposes of the new organization was its president, Taft. His conversion to the use of force, even in the limited form advocated by the League to Enforce Peace, was surprising for he had been a lifelong and active advocate of the judicial approach to world peace. He had not favored military force as an arm of the peace movement before 1915, and even then he continued to assert that an effective international court was the most necessary move toward establishing world peace. Force, he conceded, might have to be used in certain situations, but, he cautioned, "Let us get the court before we insist on the sheriff."[34] When the League adopted recourse to force as a part of its program, Taft was at first astonished and continued to be restrained in his endorsement of the theory. "It may turn out to be impracticable," he added, "but it contains some snap."[35]

In an article for the *Independent* discussing the proposed League to Enforce Peace just before its organizational meeting in 1915, Taft clarified his ideas as to the requisites for peace. He listed four requirements in the order of their importance: (1) A court capable of deciding justiciable questions between nations; (2) A Commission of Conciliation for the consideration and recommendation of a solution of all non-justiciable questions between members of the League; (3) Periodic conferences to agree upon principles of international law not already established; (4) Agreement among members of the League that if any member resorted to war without first employing the good offices of the court or the commission, the remaining members "agree to join in the forcible defense of the member thus prematurely attacked." This view, it can be seen, was in sharp contrast to the ideas of Roosevelt, especially his idea of immediate military reprisal against territorial aggression.[36]

After he became president of the League and the continuation of the war in Europe began to arouse the martial spirit of the American people, Taft became much more outspoken, but still far from specific, in advocating the use of force. "We call for a primitive political organization of the world, affording judicial and mediating agencies and an international police to stamp out the beginning of every riot of world violence. . . . Nothing but force can cure the brutality and ruthlessness of force." He derided the idea, frequently supported by opponents of the League, that the use of force by an international organization was analogous to war or was nothing more than a military alliance.[37] But Taft, for all of his bellicose statements in 1917 and 1918, probably never abandoned the idea, to which he eventually returned, that the judicial approach to peace was fundamental and the addition of a minimum of force might make it function more effectively.

Taft's overstatement of the League's determination to use force apparently was fairly typical of its leaders. Herbert S. Houston, New York publisher and Chairman of the Committee of Information for the League to Enforce Peace, for example, emphasized that peace must be put on a war footing. "It must have for its symbol the strong, farseeing eagle rather than the tame and ineffective dove." The League to Enforce Peace, he declared, stood for the theory that peace has always been made and kept "by the superior power of superior members acting in unity for the common good." The time therefore had come for the nations to guarantee peace "by all known and available sanctions at their command. . . ." But the apparently unlimited use of force Houston qualified sharply in the remainder of his speech. He would use force only to bring nations to arbitrate their disputes; economic sanctions would supply all the force necessary.[38]

A number of prominent leaders in both political parties endorsed the limited program of the League to Enforce Peace. One of these, Senator Henry Cabot Lodge, declared in 1916, in a statement destined to haunt him for years, that the use of force might "not solve the problems of peace but it cannot be otherwise. . . . We must find some way in which the united forces of the nation would be put behind the cause of peace and law."[39]

Equally significant, in terms of the later debate on the League of Nations, were the prominent leaders who rejected flatly even the limited scope of the League to Enforce Peace. Among Republicans the most noteworthy dissenters were Elihu Root and Theodore Roosevelt. Root was offered high office in the League and subjected to the persuasive arts of its leaders on many occasions but resisted all attempts to identify his name with the organization. The American people, Root was convinced, would never submit to compulsory arbitration or honor a pledge to compel other states to arbitrate disputes.[40] At the other extreme stood Roosevelt, ardent disciple of force, who dismissed the League to Enforce Peace as an impractical scheme providing that "everything shall be arbitrated everywhere." The League, complained the righteous Roosevelt, would not go to war against a nation that did wrong but only against a nation that refused to arbitrate wrong.[41] Hence, the three best known Republican statesmen, Taft, Root, and Roosevelt, represented in 1915 three widely divergent opinions on the use of force although all advocated a league of some sort.

A number of objections to the League typical of the beliefs of the peace societies were illustrated in the views of Alpheus H. Snow, one of the leaders of the Lake Mohonk Conference on International Arbitration. The use of force among nations, said Snow, was impractical in several respects: it would amount to universal war accompanied by universal ruin; it was paradoxical to pretend that conciliation, the free meeting of disputants in agreement, could ever be imposed by force against the will of a nation; the League in using force was nothing more than an alliance for it lacked any legislative or executive power; it was futile to attempt to add compulsive processes to voluntary and co-operative organizations.[42] Furthermore, it was dangerous and fallacious to accept the League's argument that the threat of force would obviate the need to use actual force.

On the Democratic side, the most prominent opponent of the League to Enforce Peace was William Jennings Bryan. At the annual peace convention at Lake Mohonk, New York, in 1916, the Great Commoner foreshadowed in a statement on American objections to enforcing peace many of the basic arguments used frequently in the subsequent debate on the League of Nations. First, Bryan castigated the League to Enforce Peace as essentially an entangling alliance, the contradiction of traditional American foreign policy instituted by George Washington. No plan that proposed to connect the United States and Europe and so involve the New World in the ancient quarrels of the Old could ever gain the support of the American people. Second, the pledge to intervene in the affairs of Europe would nullify the Monroe Doctrine, for the United States could no longer object to European intervention in the affairs of the Western Hemisphere. Third, the right of Congress to declare war would, under a league, be turned over to "a council controlled by European nations." This drastic violation of tradition could be accomplished only by an amendment to the Constitution. Any amendment made on war powers, declared Bryan, should be one providing for a popular referendum before war could be declared. The United States should not "go blindfolded into an agreement of unknown extent and effect"; it should not surrender into the hands of a foreign council the right to determine when this nation should take up arms. Fourth, the reliance in the League on military rather than moral force was a "step down." It was incompatible with the traditions of the United States in foreign affairs. "I prefer," asserted Bryan, "to have this nation a moral power in the world rather than a policeman."[43]

As may be judged from these arguments, the League to Enforce Peace by its endorsement of force, even on a strictly qualified basis, divided the peace movement irrevocably. The American Peace Society, while altering its earlier stand against supporting American participation in the First World War, held to the theory of moral sanctions alone. It refused to support the League to Enforce Peace, which had tied around its neck "at the outset the millstone of physical force."[44] Joining the American Peace Society in this opinion were the World Court League, the Church Peace Union, and the American Institute of International Law. The combined membership of these societies, however, was much smaller and included fewer national leaders than that of the League to Enforce Peace.

Implicit in the thinking of leaders of the peace movement in the United States was cultural imperialism. They persisted in attempting to project the American democratic traditions in domestic government into the realm of international affairs and to insist that it could be made to work among all people regardless of their traditions. American governmental theory argued against the use of force, for many experts believed coercive powers had not been important in the growth of the Republic.

Probably the most detailed and well-documented exposition of these theories was that made by James Brown Scott, a noted international lawyer and later a legal advisor to the American delegation at Versailles, in his work for the Carnegie Peace Foundation, *James Madison's Notes of Debates in the Federal Convention of 1787 and Their Relation to a More Perfect Society of Nations*. Here Scott developed the thesis that the American states in adopting the Constitution had founded a government on law with no recourse to force. The Federal government maintained peace between states through the agency of law, as represented in the Supreme Court. The central government exercised its authority on individuals rather than states. Military coercion was not approved as an agent of internal government by the founding fathers. Madison declared that "the more he reflected on the use of force, the more he doubted the practicability, the justice and the efficacy of it when applied to a people collectively, and not individually." A Union of States based on coercive power provided for its own destruction because the use of force against a state would be virtually a declaration of war, rather than a punitive action. It would probably be considered by the state attacked as just grounds for the dissolution of all previous compacts by which it might be bound. Out of the deliberations of the convention, Scott contended, developed the conviction—Madison called it an axiom of political science—that "the practicability of making laws, with coercive sanctions, for the States as political bodies, had been exploded on all hands." From these and many other examples, Brown concluded that the United States government was a perfect model for a world organization, resting for enforcement on the sanctity of law. One question remained: "Will the sovereign states of the Society of Nations obstinately refuse to follow the path beaten out and marked by the sovereign States of the New World, which recognized that between diplomacy and war, which they renounced, there is only war? What the States of the New World have done, the nations of the Old World can afford to consider."

There was much dissatisfaction with the programs of peace societies in the United States, but the number of societies and persons opposing any use of military force, although declining, was still large. With the growing group that advocated "enforcing peace" the theory of coercion was popular so long as it remained general and vague, both as to methods and applications. It would be fair to state that the limited use of force to accomplish arbitration, advocated by the League to Enforce Peace, represented the extreme position of the great majority of Americans who supported the use of force at all. Certainly the League was the only organized American body of significant size that advocated any use of force.

The search for peace was, of course, not exclusively an American quest. It was world-wide in scope. The proposals made in Great Britain, because of the close personal ties between men like James Bryce and Theodore Marburg or Colonel House and Robert Cecil, carried the greatest impact on Americans. The British, while they talked of using force, developed their most important proposals for peace around the idea of delaying the outbreak of hostilities by providing machinery for conferences. One of the most influential individual British advocates of a league for peace

was Lord Robert Cecil, who was active in developing
plans before the end of the war and who served as a British
delegate to the peace conference. He, in fact, gave the
league idea its first real impetus with the British government by presenting the cabinet in 1916 a memorandum on
the subject. A league, he insisted, must have adequate
sanctions, but he specified that coercion was to be used only
to compel recourse to conference. An international tribunal backed by international force he dismissed as "un-
practical." In rejecting the idea of an international army
and relying in the main on public opinion to bring compliance with the decisions of the league, Cecil closely ap-
proximated the position of the League to Enforce Peace.
His major objective, and it may be taken as representing
to a large extent the position of the more advanced advocates
of force in Britain, was a league providing for "delay and
discussion."[45]

As in the United States, there were many dissenters
who felt that even this program went too far. Undoubtedly
there were very few leaders in the government who wished
to jeopardize the sovereignty of the British government by
making it accountable to an international body capable of
enforcing its decisions or who wished to assume for the
British navy the responsibility for helping discharge against
other nations the decisions of such a body.

From this brief survey emerge two facts of utmost
significance to the future of the League of Nations incorporating the mutual guarantee of Article Ten: first, the weight
of popular American tradition in foreign policy was against
any permanent, binding commitment to employ military
intervention to maintain world peace; second, in the general
approval for some sort of league for peace the question of
the use of force divided the peacemakers into numerous
irreconcilable and ineffectual factions. The majority stood
between the extremes of pacifism and militarism, favoring
the theory of enforcement but limiting sharply the use of
sanctions in practice. Establishment of a league capable of
executing its decisions against its members would have been
in 1919-1920 nothing short of a revolution in American
foreign policy and in world politics. Successful revolutions
are compounded of overwhelming popular conviction, sharp-

ened by repeated repression, and tempered to sacrifice under the inspiration of zealous leaders. The first requisite, popular conviction, was lacking in 1920. The theory of the Wilson revolution was that national security could be achieved only by collective action made effective at the cost of national sovereignty. Regardless of the merits of this theory, it cannot be shown that there was widespread popular support for it, although there was a great popular demand for peace. The leader of the revolution for collective security would find his followers undisciplined, uncertain, and fainthearted.

CHAPTER II

Woodrow Wilson and the Origins of Article Ten

THE eventual leader of the 1919 revolution in American foreign affairs was Woodrow Wilson. Wilson had never been a student of international relations and during his first term as President showed relatively little interest in becoming one. Yet in common with many leaders of opinion the general ideal of a world organization for peace attracted him. He did not, however, definitely express approval of military force for this purpose, even in private conversations, until late in 1914, but shortly thereafter the idea began to take hold of him. Before the end of the year he evolved a radical expression of it which was little altered during the remainder of his career—the provision for a mutual guarantee of political and territorial integrity under democratic government (the prototype of Article Ten) publicly endorsed in the abortive Pan-American Treaty of 1915. He began to assume a position of leadership in the movement to enforce peace in May, 1916, when he gave formal public approval to the general principle of an international organization incorporating coercive powers. Later in the year, during his campaign for the presidency Wilson sought in a few speeches to educate the public to the general responsibilities that he felt the United States must assume in the new world order.

His relative lack of interest in and attention to foreign affairs no doubt led Wilson to simplify the problems and accept the belief that a single formula could solve all of them. This formula, so his knowledge and veneration of the American system of government led him to believe, was the projection of American political theory to world politics. The fundamental responsibility of the Federal government had been to provide people with an opportunity to create a local government of their own choosing and to guarantee its existence. These ideas, of course, were expressed in both* the Articles of Confederation and the Constitution. In the former the states bound themselves to "assist each other against all force offered to or attacks made upon them or any of them." In the latter the United States undertook to guarantee every state a republican form of government and protect it from invasion. Transferring American experience to international affairs, Wilson maintained from his first to his last statements on the subject that the primary requisite of a league of nations was a guarantee, by the use of force if necessary, of the political and territorial integrity of all member nations. Justice must be upheld internationally and nationally, but without a guarantee a league would be powerless to halt aggressive war or a breach of justice.[1]

In short, Wilson's approach to a league of nations was imbued with the American spirit of manifest destiny. The nation had been growing and developing for a century, Wilson declared, in order to serve as an example, both on the domestic and the international scene, to the politically bankrupt systems of Europe. Wilson did not seek the establishment of an association of nations so much as the founding of a universal school for the world to share America's political wisdom. "The commands of democracy," he said in 1916, "are as imperative as its privileges and opportunities are wide and generous. Its compulsion is upon us. It will be great and lift a great light for the guidance of the nations only if we are great and carry that light high and for the guidance of our own feet. We are not worthy to stand here unless we ourselves be indeed and in truth real democrats and servants of mankind, ready to give our very lives for the freedom and justice and spiritual exaltation of the great nation which shelters and nurtures us."[2] Wilson's approach to peace, though typically American, was less than flattering to Europeans. They did not recognize his right to catalogue their sins and to preach repentance. Despite his good intentions his fundamental view on peace was to offend nearly all of the statesmen he met at the Paris Peace Conference.[3]

Wilson was not aware of the European reaction to his plans, but he recognized, as a politician of keen perception, that his program would meet its most serious opposition

in the Senate and from the American people. His potential
followers would be bound by the paralyzing power of comfortable and tested traditions, discouraged by the popular
repugnance for any new and dangerous responsibilities. Uncertain as to what course might arouse the necessary popular
support, Wilson remained cautious, seeking approval of the
general idea before announcing a specific plan for peace.

In 1915 Wilson first moved to translate his general ideals
on world peace into a specific plan with a regional pact—
a Pan-American Treaty. Its first article provided a positive
guarantee of the territorial and political integrity of the
signatory nations under a democratic form of government.
The idea, however, did not originate with Wilson, although
it paralleled his thinking.

Historical precedent, almost a century old, foreshadowed
the mutual guarantee. The first Inter-American Conference,
held in 1826, sought to stabilize boundaries under the guarantee and protection of a proposed confederation. No
signatory was to declare war on another without first in-
voking the conciliatory decision of the general assembly of
the confederation. Similar guarantees were a part of three
other Latin American pacts, all unsuccessful. The United
States in 1881 and again in 1890 joined Pan-American states
in unsuccessful attempts to make illegal any conquest or
cession of territory achieved by the threat of war.[4] Brazil
continued the effort and introduced to the Hague Conference in 1907 a proposal making it illegal to alter national
boundaries without first seeking arbitration. Later a Trans-
Mississippi Congress called for a joint agreement by the
various governments of America for a mutual guarantee
of their sovereignty and territorial integrity.[5]

All new world plans for peace involved the Monroe
Doctrine. The United States interpreted the Doctrine as
affording territorial integrity to South American states and
obviating the need for additional machinery of peace. South
American states, however, had grown to regard the Doctrine's protection as an insult to their maturity, if not a
menace to their existence. In the United States a few
intellectual leaders condemned the Doctrine as obsolete,
and in Congress, despite the fact that such radical suggestions
were generally unpopular, James L. Slayden of Texas pro-

posed reinterpreting the Monroe Doctrine in terms of the century-long search for territorial security. His resolutions of April 4, 1911, adopted by the National Peace Association, and of April 23, 1913, provided for a "joint agreement between the various Governments of America for the mutual guaranty of their sovereignty and territorial integrity. . . ."[6] Here in the positive guarantee was the core of Wilson's Pan-American Pact and of Article Ten of the League Covenant. Congress, however, was not impressed; the resolution was tabled with no debate. Apparently, Slayden's work was unnoted by Wilson at the time. After Wilson outlined a new Latin American program in his 1913 Mobile speech, Secretary of State Bryan sent the President a letter from Congressman Slayden, urging, in a sharply modified version of his earlier resolution, a negative guarantee—the nations simply pledged themselves not to violate their neighbor's territory.[7] In Latin America, Perez Triana, former Colombian minister to Great Britain and a member of the Hague Court of Arbitration, in January, 1914, also attempted, in a resolution brought to Wilson's attention, to provide a mutual guarantee.[8]

Meanwhile, the principle of mutual military guarantee of territory was urged upon Wilson in 1914 by a number of Americans. Among these was Charles W. Eliot, former president of Harvard University, who sent the President a plan for a military alliance of the great powers based on the use of force—"indispensable for the present protection of civilization against a savagery, and for the future establishment and maintenance of federal relations and peace among the nations of Europe."[9] Among Wilson's close advisors, notably Colonel House and Secretary Bryan, some form of guarantee of territory was gaining acceptance. House advocated as early as August 14, 1914, a general proposal for territorial integrity.[10] It became part of a positive policy which House, who wished Wilson to take a more active role in foreign affairs, developed to present to the President at an opportune moment. Secretary of State Bryan urged upon the President a negative guarantee under which all nations agreed to denounce aggressive war and to respect existing boundaries. Andrew Carnegie urged Wilson "to banish war from the American continent" through the estab-

lishment of a league of twenty-one American republics as
an "example to the world." The President thanked Carnegie
for "lodging the idea in his mind."[11] Theodore Roosevelt
reached Wilson through an article in the *New York Times*
in October of 1914 advocating a league based on military
force. The President's later references in speeches indicated
familiarity with an approval of Roosevelt's suggestions.[12]
Thus, by December, 1914, when House suggested a Pan-
American Pact, Wilson was familiar with the arguments
favoring a system of military sanctions as the requisite
insuring a peaceful world.

In his own mind Wilson conceived of force in international affairs as comparable to its use in the domestic
community, where police power, though always available, is
needed in marginal cases only. The vast majority of domestic
disputes are settled by peaceful means; there is no continual
contest of arms. The most vital element in the American
system, Wilson believed, is not physical force but moral
force and public opinion: "I believe that the glory of
America is that she is a great spiritual conception" and "the
one thing that the world cannot permanently resist is the
moral force of great and triumphant convictions." At the
same time he insisted that all government rested ultimately
on physical force.[13]

Sometime between August and October of 1914 Wilson
reached a definite conclusion: "No nation shall ever again
be permitted to acquire an inch of land by conquest."
Force must be brought to bear through an association of
nations capable of administering punishment by war against
aggressor nations.[14] House, on December 16, suggested a
loose league of American states to "guarantee security from
aggression and furnish a mechanism for the pacific settlement of disputes" and to serve as a model of international
cooperation for the European states.[15]

After hearing these suggestions Wilson was eager to
act, and wrote immediately the nexus of the Pan-American
Treaty: "mutual guarantees of political independence under
republican form of government and mutual guarantees of
territorial integrity."[16] As written in final form Article One
read: "The high contracting parties to this solemn covenant
and agreement hereby join one another in a common and

mutual guarantee of territorial integrity and of political independence under republican forms of government." This was Wilson's first official endorsement of the ideal later to become Article Ten.[17]

As if to follow the classic form of drama, a foreshadowing of doom was present at the birth of Article Ten. Chile objected to the pact immediately, largely because of the mutual guarantee of territorial and political integrity. Wilson declined to compromise for, as he told Bryan, compromise on the guarantee would destroy the value of the Pact.[18]

Despite Wilson's enthusiasm, by August of 1916 the Pan-American Pact was dying. Even Colonel House was willing to bury it by October of that year. The negotiations, undertaken as a model for a European peace settlement, dragged to final failure in 1917, a model followed all too closely. The Pact's Article One, however, was a significant model, "the immediate prototype of the Covenant of the League of Nations."[19]

The Pan-American Pact focused Wilson's attention on methods for maintaining peace. To the sanctions of international law, moral force, and public opinion there must be added, he concluded, that of military force. Yet, he feared that the American public was not prepared for such a project.[20]

Throughout 1915 plans for peace with general programs for enforcement were suggested to Wilson many times. Lord Edward Grey, for one, insisted that wars might be prevented in the future by an association of nations powerful enough to punish those breaking its rules. These ideas Colonel House, who was in close contact with Grey, relayed to Wilson.[21]

Wilson's plan for a guaranteed peace was influenced by his unsuccessful attempts in 1915 and 1916 to bring about a settlement of the war. When diplomatic negotiations failed, Wilson felt it imperative to renew his efforts through a public address demanding a conference to end the European war and outlining the basis of an enduring peace. An appropriate occasion offered itself in an invitation to speak to a Washington meeting of the League to Enforce Peace. The President devoted much time to what he realized was a most vital address and quite possibly a turning point

in American history. In his own mind he was convinced
that the American policy of isolation was doomed, as the
natural result of America's rise to world power and the
inexorable trend of historical development throughout the
ages toward an all-embracing world community.

The first step in moving from isolation to responsible
world citizenship was the extension to the entire world of a
guarantee of peace similar to that written into the unsuccessful Pan-American Pact. To the pacifist American Union
Against Militarism, Wilson declared, May 8: "In the last
analysis the peace of society is obtained by force, and when
action comes,—it comes by opinion, but back of opinion is
the ultimate application of force. . . . If you say, 'We
shall not have any war,' you have got to have the force
to make that 'shall' bite." This was not a militaristic idea, the
President hastened to add, for military force was to be applied by a combination of states.[22] A few days later Wilson
wrote House that the United States in its program for peace
must insist on "a universal alliance to maintain freedom of
the seas and to prevent any war begun either (a) contrary
to treaty covenants or (b) without warning and full inquiry,—a virtual guarantee of territorial integrity and
political independence."[23]

Wilson's final draft of the speech did not reflect his
unequivocal endorsement of military force for peace. House,
who wrote one complete draft for the speech, advised
glossing over the specific problem of enforcing peace.
Politically, it would be wiser to work for general acceptance
of a league as the necessary first step. Robert Lansing also
strongly urged deletion of all reference to physical force.[24]
The Secretary of State, it should be noted, opposed military
sanction in principle and predicted at this time that it was
a dangerous doctrine politically, for the Senate and the
American people would never accept a peace organization
incorporating the obligation of a positive guarantee. The
guarantee presented too definite a threat to American independence and sovereignty. As a consequence Wilson's
public statement was much milder than his private convictions and appeared to be practically in agreement with the
aims of the League to Enforce Peace. Actually his plans for
peace required a far more drastic break with tradition than
the League charter contemplated.

Wilson's speech, an important milestone in the progress of Article Ten, was described as the most important statement on American foreign policy since the announcement of the Monroe Doctrine. He emphasized the right of every nation to choose the sovereignty under which it should live, the right of small states to enjoy the same respect for their sovereignty and territorial integrity that great powers insisted upon, and the right of the world to be free from every disturbance of peace stemming from aggression or disregard for the rights of nations. In essence the President demanded an end to isolation and an assumption by America of the responsibility of partnership in an "association of nations formed to realize common objectives" and "make them secure against violation." Wilson assumed that war was the result of injustice instigated by aggressors easily identifiable in every case. The association of nations, he asserted, must punish aggression with a "common force," and by "coercion" maintain order, "safeguard right," and afford a "virtual guarantee of territorial integrity and political independence."

Hamilton Holt through the pages of the *Independent* hailed Wilson's address as of importance "hardly possible to exaggerate," calling it a "Declaration of Interdependence." However, a great part of the significance that Holt saw in Wilson's speech was evidence of unity among the leaders of the peace movement. Just before the President delivered the speech Holt printed concise statements on the League to Enforce Peace by Roosevelt, Taft, and Wilson in parallel columns in the *Independent*. These statements, Holt asserted, would "show the unanimity in aim and method of the three men. . . ." Yet, as these very examples demonstrated, there was more disagreement than agreement in the theories of the three men. Wilson proposed a political league of all nations with all nations participating in military enforcement of peace. Taft stressed a court with enforcement of arbitration, while Roosevelt called for military sanction imposed by the great powers alone.[25] Holt emphasized, nevertheless, that in Wilson's philosophizing on principles and the League's stressing of "ways and means" there was little difference.[26] The President had endorsed the League to Enforce Peace. The determination by advocates of peace organizations to see unity where little fundamental agreement ex-

isted was to persist and so give rise to the charge that Taft
and Roosevelt in their later opposition to Wilson's League
were directed by political expediency to a denial of their
own convictions. If leaders differed, so too must their followers disagree.

Wilson's awareness of potential opposition led him to
announce only general principles. He refused also to let
even the nebulous plan outlined at Washington be presented to Congress formally, as Taft urged, for approval
in a joint resolution. Membership in any active association
of nations, the President feared, would meet rejection in
Congress.[27] Apparently he was right. Senators immediately
objected that Wilson's association of nations was, in fact,
an entangling alliance—anathema in American foreign policy.
Abroad the reaction was no more encouraging. The British
and French paid little attention to Wilson's suggestion and
showed no enthusiasm for a league that could guarantee
peace. The handwriting was beginning to appear on the
wall.

Throughout the rest of 1916 Wilson was preoccupied
with the problems of office and the burden of campaigning
for re-election. The Democratic party platform, as did the
Republican, gave general endorsement to his May 27 speech
advocating an association of nations. But Wilson did not
make a league a major campaign issue. Following the politically sound advice of House, Wilson in his advocacy of a
league avoided specific plans, while emphasizing the American determination to see justice prevail throughout the world
by employing physical as well as moral force to back up the
"opinions of mankind."[28] Nevertheless, he sought to prepare
the way for a league by exhorting the electorate to recognize
that for the new era just beginning, America's traditional
foreign policy would be inadequate. It must be altered to
meet the demands of America's destiny.

"You have heard of the Monroe Doctrine, gentlemen
. . . . we stand here with the glorious power of this country,
ready to swing it out into the field of action wherever
liberty and independence and political integrity are threatened anywhere in the Western Hemisphere. And we are
ready—nobody has authorized me to say this, but I am sure
of it—we are ready to join with the other nations of the

world in seeing that the kind of justice prevails anywhere that we believe in."

In employing force for peace Wilson drew a distinction in his campaign addresses of 1916 between force as represented by "the opinion of mankind" and the force of autocratic militarism bent on selfish purposes. "Force can sometimes hold things steady until opinion has time to form but no force that was ever exerted, except in response to that opinion, was ever a conquering and predominant force." A league endorsed by all nations would use force in response to public opinion. "There must be a just and settled peace, and we here in America must contribute the full force of our enthusiasm and of our authority as a nation to the organization of that peace upon world-wide foundations . . . . No nation . . . can any longer remain neutral as against any willful disturbance of the peace of the world. . . . The nations of the world must unite in joint guarantees that whatever is done to disturb the whole world's life must first be tested in the court of the whole world's opinion before it is attempted."

Responsibilities of world citizenship could no longer be evaded. Washington's advice on entangling alliances, said Wilson, was to avoid entanglement in the "ambitions and national purposes of other nations. It does not mean . . . that we are to avoid the entanglements of the world, for we are part of the world, and nothing that concerns the whole world can be indifferent to us." Destiny decreed American participation in a world federation. "I have said, and shall say again, that when the great present war is over it will be the duty of America to join with the other nations of the world in some kind of a league for the maintenance of peace. . . . We are saving ourselves in order that we may unite in that final league of nations in which it shall be understood that there is no neutrality where any nation is doing wrong, in that final league of nations which must, in the providence of God, come into the world where nation shall be leagued with nation in order to show all mankind that no man may lead any nation into acts of aggression without having all the other nations of the world leagued against it."

In Wilson's conception, the league of nations was definitely to be based on military force, for he emphasized, "America is going to take this position, . . . she will lend her moral influence, not only, but her physical force, if other nations will join her, to see to it that no nation and no group of nations tries to take advantage of another nation or group of nations, and that the only thing ever fought for is the common rights of humanity. . . . America must hereafter be ready as a member of the family of nations to exert her whole force, moral and physical, to the assertion of those rights throughout the round globe." Many times Wilson acknowledged that his was a new policy, for "the world will never be again what it has been. . . . America up to the present time has been, as if by deliberate choice, confined and provincial. Henceforth, she belongs to the world and must act as part of the world, and all of the attitudes of Americans will henceforth be altered. American purposes are going to be tested by the purposes of mankind, and not by the purposes of national ambition."[29]

Wilson realized that his proposal was radically new. What he failed to calculate correctly was the state of public opinion. Blinded by his own enthusiasm and sense of urgency he interpreted the war-spurred popular interest of the people in international affairs and the general talk in favor of world organization not as indications of slight change but as evidence of final adjustment. America was eager to take an active role in world affairs. There were many objections to a strong league able to enforce its decisions. Indeed, "nearly every major argument in the later League fight was advanced *before* Woodrow Wilson spoke in favor of any League!"[30] But the degree of objection was difficult to gauge, for only complete realization of the radical scope of Wilson's plans turned erstwhile advocates of an association of nations against the League of Nations in 1919-1920. There was a deep and fundamental issue to be decided, a single covenant to be drafted to the satisfaction of men of widely divergent convictions.

CHAPTER III

Wilson's Preparations for the Peace Conference

BACK of the generalities of campaign oratory Wilson carried in his own mind the firm conviction that a league must grow by precedent and experience from the mutual pledge to guarantee territorial and political integrity. Always more intrigued with the spirit of the law than the letter, he spent little time on the practical problem of executing such a guarantee and completed only one draft of a league by the time he left in the fall of 1918 for the peace conference. Even so, the critical years in Wilson's revolution in foreign policy were not 1918 to 1920 when the battle was joined but 1916 to 1918 when he had to mobilize his forces.

The announcements of his fundamental ideal—the expansion of the Monroe Doctrine into a world-wide guarantee —were flatly rejected by important senators. Such public support as he won was largely superficial, compounded more of ignorance and war-inspired idealism than of understanding and sober dedication. During the two years before the peace conference, he was not able to lay the political groundwork for acceptance of the League by overcoming popular or senatorial opposition to the first principle, the mutual guarantee. Thus, the fight for Article Ten, for the type league Wilson felt essential to the expression of America's new role in world affairs, was largely lost before he committed any of his celebrated "mistakes" of 1918. A great barrier of inertia and tradition which he shook but could not move blocked Wilson's way to world leadership.

Why was Wilson unable to build up a favorable backing for his plan during these critical years? It is certainly true that the President was sorely pressed for time and that many problems of war demanded immediate attention while peace was still a matter of the future. But more important in accounting for his relative inactivity on the League issue was his conviction, upheld by his political advisors, that his program for peace would meet with sharp opposition at home. His potential followers, the leader of the revolution knew, would be bound by the paralyzing power of comfortable and tested traditions, discouraged by the popular repugnance for any new and possibly dangerous responsibilities.

Apparently Wilson decided that his best hope lay, not in gradually leading the people to accept the new program over which much controversy might develop, but in presenting them with a completed proposal, an accomplished fact. In any event, he made no effort beyond very general statements to educate the public. He did not want the details of various league plans published in 1918; he did not explain in detail his own program to the American people until his September 1919 tour, when the deadlock in the Senate forced his hand. Thus, he chose to depend for success on the weight of the popular emotional desire for peace rather than on developing a reasoned understanding of the machinery of a league. As has been noted often, Wilson throughout the war emphasized the idealistic causes for American participation—saving democracy, fighting a war to end war—rather than the practical reason of national security. There was the same emphasis on ideals in his peace campaign: duty, responsibility, a just peace that would complete the humanitarian objectives of the war. Wilson employed diplomacy in peace and military strategy in war to achieve his ideal aims as closely as did European diplomats in their quest for realistic goals. Unfortunately for Wilson, he had to win popular approval for his program. The urgency and emotional impact of the martial spirit supported the passage of war measures. In the more leisurely and emotionally relaxed atmosphere of peacetime it was far more difficult, if not wholly impossible, to get public support for unselfish idealism as a national program.

Moreover, Wilson was cautious in the years 1916-1918 because Senate opposition to the mutual guarantee was definite and clear. Remembering the Senate's consistent nullification or rejection of arbitration treaties, one had no reason to expect its attitude to have been otherwise. Wilson's actions, 1916-1918, and his few recorded comments indicate that he had little hope of the Senate ever endorsing a league for peace backed by coercive powers. Certainly Lansing, his secretary of state, was of that opinion and advised abandonment or radical modification of the mutual guarantee. But Wilson was unwilling to yield. Instead, he moved toward a policy, which he had used in domestic legislation, of forcing his program through in spite of Congress.

Other leaders probably would have given up the whole program or settled for a part of it, but it was never Wilson's nature to compromise where principle was at stake. He thought in terms of sweeping reforms; he was unwilling to accept partial programs. Further, by philosophy and temperament he cast the President in the dominant role in all matters, especially in foreign affairs, where he considered the President's control "very absolute." In the management of treaties in particular, the President did not have to disclose any step of negotiations until the whole was complete. "When in any critical matter it is completed the government is virtually committed. Whatever its disinclinations, the Senate may feel itself committed also."[1] These thoughts, written a decade before the League crisis, were Wilson's convictions in 1917 for they describe the policy he followed in regard to the League during the critical years 1916-1918.

Wilson's major pre-conference effort to launch a league came late in 1916 as a part of another of his attempts to halt the European war. The public and Senate disapproval halted Wilson's efforts. This time rather than send House to Europe once more, Wilson determined to appeal to the powers through identic notes asking that they state the terms on which they could make peace. During late November and early December he concentrated on writing this note. In his first draft, November 27, he asserted: "A common object has been professed by the leaders of the governments at war, viz. such a league to enforce peace as will make the future secure." And later in this draft he revealed his determination "to effect a league of nations based upon a peace which shall be guaranteed against breach by the common force and an intelligent organization of the common interest."[2]

While composing the note Wilson reconsidered the

practicability of enforcing peace. The newspapers carried a great deal of unfavorable comment on the association of nations. The basic question, raised many times, was the impossibility of reconciling the Monroe Doctrine with a world league. A league enforcing peace must authorize European intervention in the Western Hemisphere. For a time the President even considered dropping the whole theory of physical coercion in favor of peace enforced by moral suasion alone.[3] Eventually he decided to stand by physical force but to minimize its importance in the new world order. At the same time he reached the definite conclusion that the Monroe Doctrine was not in conflict with a world league empowered to enforce peace.

In the final version of the note he emphasized the interest of the United States in measures to secure peace and relieve weaker powers of the perils of wrong and violence. As to guarantees, the American people, said Wilson, "stand ready, and even eager, to cooperate in the accomplishment of these ends, when the war is over, with every influence and resource at their command."[4]

But even this much modified statement was too strong for many senators. Borah led a full-scaled attack on the basic idea of a league charging it could never be reconciled with American tradition.[5] So bitter was the opposition that Hitchcock after four attempts to get endorsement of a resolution approving Wilson's proposal was forced to delete all reference to a league. Even then there were seventeen votes against the resolution with thirty-one abstaining from voting. The proposal, even in general terms, to enter a world alliance to keep peace collectively was distasteful to an important group of senators. Truly could Wilson write on January 17, ". . . it is hard to see how to guide Congress successfully."[6] Wilson's fear of Congressional opposition to a league, apparent as early as his first address on May 27, was definitely confirmed.

Meanwhile, his identic notes had found no more hospitable reception abroad than they had at home. Despite congressional opposition and the growing hostility of the future allies, Wilson determined to make yet another effort, this time in a speech to the Senate, to force agreement among the belligerents on the terms of peace and keep America out of war by ending the conflict. His personal conviction that force must be employed to achieve permanent peace was clearly shown in his shorthand preliminary notes for this speech: "Our interest only in the law and such justice as it was supposed international law had secured—Our whole moral, and if necessary physical, force ready to be used to sustain these." Wilson's advisors sought, as they had done before, to make these references to force less specific in the final draft. At Lansing's suggestion, for example, the President altered the definite phrase "a league to enforce peace" to a general statement, "a league to insure peace."

But so revolutionary was Wilson's plan that its fundamentally inescapable challenge to traditional interpretations could not be hidden. Therefore, much of the address of January 22 to the Senate and, in Wilson's phrase, "to the peoples of the world," was devoted to showing that a "League for Peace" insuring justice would not breach "our traditions or our policy" but was indeed "a fulfillment . . . of all that we have professed or striven for." Borah and others feared a league might destroy the Monroe Doctrine. On the contrary, Wilson argued that the League drew its basic principle of enforcing peace from the Doctrine.

"I am proposing, as it were, that the nations . . . adopt the doctrine of President Monroe as the doctrine of the world: that no nation should seek to extend its polity over any other nation or people, but that every people should be left free to determine its own policy, its own way of development, unhindered, unthreatened, unafraid, the little along with the great and powerful.

"I am proposing that all nations henceforth avoid entangling alliances which would draw them into competitions of power. . . . There is no entangling alliance in a concert of power. . . . These are American principles, American policies. . . . They are the principles of mankind and must prevail."[7]

The President did not minimize the effort that would be necessary to make the principles of mankind prevail. "It will be absolutely necessary that a force be created as a guarantor of the permanency of the settlement so much greater than the force of any nation now engaged or any alliance hitherto formed or projected that no nation, no probable combination of nations could face or withstand it. If the peace presently to be made is to endure, it must be a peace made secure by the organized major force of mankind."

This January 22 statement to the Senate on the terms of peace was a formal expansion of the position taken by Wilson in his May 27 speech to the League to Enforce Peace. It is significant that even at this early date a league, in Wilson's thinking, was inseparable from a peace treaty, for it must be the very basis of any satisfactory peace settlement. Later Wilson was to find political reasons for combining the League and the Treaty, although they had in fact never been separated in his own mind. Significant, too, in the growth of Article Ten was Wilson's emphasis in the January 22 address on the guarantee of "territorial integrity," in the sense of protecting peoples rather than lands from conquest. In this fashion he tied the mutual guarantee to the American principle of government by the consent of the governed. Monroe in the Doctrine had emphasized the differences between the Old and the New World; Wilson would eliminate those differences by gaining European acceptance of the new-world principles of non-aggression and self-determination for "every people."[8]

In the history of Article Ten, January 22, 1917, was a crucial day. If the move to end American isolation required nothing more than a broadening of well-established American traditions and European acceptance of them, the step might be made easily. But immediately senators challenged the thesis of easy transition and protested that the new wine of internationalism could not be contained in the old bottles of nationalism. Only a few days after Wilson's speech Borah introduced a resolution stating the traditional foreign policies of the United States as announced by Washington, Jefferson, and Monroe and calling on the Senate to reaffirm the worth and wisdom of these policies.[9] Such a resolution, had the Senate adopted it, would have ended immediately any possibility of American participation in Wilson's proposed "League for Peace" backed by the organized major force of mankind.

The President's interpretation of the Monroe Doctrine and his proposal for a league to enforce peace also drew the

criticism of Senator Lodge in a long address delivered in the
Senate on February 28, 1917. This relatively reasoned and
dispassionate critique of the revolution in foreign affairs
showed Lodge to be opposed to the principle of mutual
guarantee long before Article Ten became a political issue.
Of course, the Senator and the President were already
bitter personal enemies. Time and again in this lengthy
discourse Lodge asserted that his only interest was "to uncover the realities which lie behind the President's proposi-
tions and to avoid 'the soft concealments' to which he justly
objects. . . ." The Monroe Doctrine, Lodge asserted, was
and never could be anything more than a regional agreement.
To attempt to apply it to the world at large, as Wilson
proposed, would destroy it. Like John Fiske's law of myths,
said Lodge, when we find the Doctrine everywhere we
may be sure it does not exist anywhere.

"If we are to abandon the Monroe Doctrine," Lodge
continued, "this is one way of doing it," for the theory of
enforcing peace involved far more than an extension of the
Doctrine. The United States heretofore had confined itself
to voluntary systems of arbitration. This system must be
abandoned, if Wilson's plan was to be followed. The use of
force could not be voluntary: "There is no halfway house to
stop at." Enforcing peace, Lodge went on to declare, was
an attractive general proposition, one that he himself had
been drawn to once. But careful consideration of issues had
forced him to conclude, "This is a matter which cannot be
determined by verbal adherence to a general principle.
Everything here depends upon the details." These details
included such problems as organizing the major force of
mankind into an army that must number not less than
5,000,000 men. The share of the United States in this vast
enterprise would be 500,000 men "to be held ready for war
at the pleasure of other nations. . . ." Peace could be enforced only by men and arms; no amount of shouting about
the blessings of peace could relieve the nation from these
obligations. Peace could not be sustained through a league
by "language alone or by moral suasion. . . ."

Again conceding that an effective league must be one
backed by force as the President described, Lodge asked:
"Are we prepared to commit ourselves to a purely general

proposition without knowing where we are going or what
is to be demanded of us, except that we shall be compelled
to furnish our quota of military and naval forces to the
service of a league in which we shall have but one voice?"
Until the American people considered at length the practical
implications of a league to enforce peace, until they were
absolutely willing to accept the tremendous obligations of
such an undertaking, they would do little service to the cause
of peace by accepting commitments they were not prepared
to discharge. These facts, Lodge said, would infuriate the
advocates of enforced peace. It might be asked "by those
who wish to have the world's peace assured by force,
without using force to do it, why conjure up these phantoms
of unpleasant possibilities? My reply is that they are not
phantoms but simply the realities which it is our duty to
uncover and upon which the whole scheme is founded."
The policy of Wilson was not an extension of the traditional policy of the nation's founders. "There is no lurking
place for a league for peace 'supported by the organized
major force of mankind' in sentences of George Washington
and Thomas Jefferson. . . ."[10] Nor was Lodge alone in these
views. Somewhat further removed from the political
scene, Elihu Root, an experienced interpreter of the Monroe
Doctrine, was complaining in his private correspondence
that Wilson knew nothing about the Monroe Doctrine
and was advocating policies that would destroy it.

Unfortunately for Wilson's Article Ten "history was on
the side of the opposition." The Doctrine was almost inseparably connected with the American traditions of neutrality and non-entanglement in European affairs. A pledge
binding the United States to intervene in European affairs
to enforce peace would render meaningless American objections to European intervention in the Western Hemisphere. The Pan-American Pact was not, despite Wilson's
hopes, a practical model for world peace. It was valid only
so long as it remained a regional agreement confined to the
area traditionally covered by the Monroe Doctrine. As
such it was in fact an extension of the Doctrine. But to apply
the Pan-American Pact's principle of mutual cooperation
in repelling territorial aggression to areas outside of North
and South America was not compatible with the Monroe

Doctrine. Wilson had the more difficult side of the argument in working for change. His opponents had the advantage of defending the status quo and, in the more or less objective opinion of historians, the more logical argument as well.[11] Article Ten had been dealt a pre-natal injury.

Wilson's January 22 appeal, eloquent though it was, did not bring the war to a close or the Senate to a league for peace. In fact, there was no single supporting speech in the Senate comparable in any way to those made against Wilson's program by Borah and Lodge. Nevertheless, Wilson continued to base his hopes for peace on a league incorporating guarantees backed by force. Early in February he returned to this theme in a memorandum stating minimum requirements for peace. The first two of the four articles dealt with guarantees of political independence and territorial integrity. The third specified a guarantee against economic warfare with the fourth calling for a limitation of armaments.[12] The President indicated on several occasions a conviction that such a program would not meet with Senate approval.

In April the United States went to war. For the time being the use of force became a practical necessity as well as an ideal goal. Wilson charged the American people to use force—"force to the utmost, force without stint or limit." Victory must be achieved, the triumph of justice secured. Then America's destiny might be fulfilled: "Once more we shall make good with our lives and fortunes the great faith to which we were born, and a new glory shall shine in the face of people." He delineated American destiny: "I have exactly the same things in mind now that I had in mind when I addressed the Senate on the twenty-second of January last. . . . Our object now, as then, is to vindicate the principles of peace and justice in the life of the world as against selfish and autocratic power and to set up amongst the really free and self-governed peoples of the world such a concert of purpose and of action as will henceforth ensure the observance of those principles." Victory would destroy "autocratic governments backed by organized force." Future peace would be guaranteed in a "partnership of democratic nations," a "league of honor, a partnership of opinion."[13] The European Allies, Wilson realized, had a very different objective. They wanted Germany "beaten and so badly beaten that there would be a dictated peace, a victorious peace." As a neutral, America could moderate these claims. He feared, now that the United States had entered the war, that the Allies would "have their way in the very thing America had hoped against and struggled against."

For a time Wilson himself seemed to narrow his ideal of a universal alliance for peace to a war instrument, a league of democratic nations bent on the destruction of autocratic militarism such as had been suggested to him by President Eliot of Harvard in 1914,[14] and was later advocated, in somewhat different form, by leaders of the League to Enforce Peace. In fact, Hamilton Holt had written in 1916 that the League to Enforce Peace might prove to be the solution to the problem of ending the war as well as to the problem of permanent peace. If agreement could be reached "as to the basis of a durable peace, then all immediate issues become relatively insignificant. . . ."[15] The hard pressed Allies did not quibble about Wilson's significant but subtle distinctions in war aims or argue that their objectives were as noble as Wilson's. Later, when the war was won, they showed resentment and satirized Wilson as a missionary who sought to "rescue the poor European heathen from their age-long worship of false and fiery gods."[16]

Despite much negotiation, including a trip to England by House, the Allies failed to reach agreement on war and peace aims during 1917. In December Wilson with the aid of House and his group of experts known as the Inquiry prepared a statement of American policy—the Fourteen Points.[17] The last point, of course, called for an association of nations authorized to guarantee political and territorial integrity to great and small states alike.

When the Allies subsequently accepted the Fourteen Points in principle as the basis of peace, Wilson felt that he had achieved a major victory in committing them to the League. Apparently satisfied with his progress Wilson made no attempt, and had made none in 1917, to work out the details of the peace organization.

The President seemed to be doing nothing to develop a peace organization himself and so little toward supporting the League to Enforce Peace that its leaders began to doubt that he really believed in the principle of force at all. Actually it was the leaders themselves—"butters-in and woolgatherers"—that Wilson disliked. Then, too, he felt they had "a very much too definite programme. . . ."[18] In a letter, read by House in 1918 to Root, Taft, and Lowell, Wilson emphasized the importance of the mutual guarantee. At the same time, he asserted that the Senate "would be unwilling to enter into an agreement by which a majority of the other nations could tell the United States when they must go to war."[19] Some leaders of the League with sharp insight suspected that Wilson, the shrewd politician, was not revealing his true position. They surmised that he accepted the use of force as the capstone of any plan for peace and was determined to enhance his political position by gaining personal control of the movement to enforce peace.[20] To this end he sought to discourage the League to Enforce Peace, dominated by Republicans, and reduce its effectiveness.

Taft, for one, became convinced that it was useless to count on Wilson, whatever his motives might be, for the time being. "This does not discourage me," Taft wrote, "because he is nothing but a weathercock, and when he finds out . . . the solidarity of the demand of the American people for . . . an organized force of the nations, he will come again to our view."[21]

Wilson continued his quiet and cautious policy. He rejected in March of 1918 a specific proposal giving to a few nations executive control to enforce an association's decisions, a plan similar to Roosevelt's. With much insight, Wilson pointed out that the Senate would never ratify any treaty which "puts the force of the United States at the disposal of any such group or body."[22] However, speaking to a group of Mexican editors in June of 1918, he said: "The whole family of nations will have to guarantee to each nation that no nation shall violate its political independence or its territorial integrity. That is the basis—the only conceivable basis—for the future peace of the world, and I must admit that I was anxious to have the states of the continents of America in the Pan-American Pact, show the way to the rest of the world as to how to make a peace."[23]

Despite these conflicting opinions in his own mind Wilson did not attempt to clarify them by drafting specific charters for a league. In fact, he declared privately that it would be a mistake to attempt to formulate a complete constitution at one time. The League idea was organic; the seed, already planted in the Fourteen Points, the solemn covenant "covering mutual guarantees of political independence and territorial integrity" must be allowed time to grow.[24] The method of translating the mutual pledge into action and the difficult question of enforcing it must be answered slowly as decisions were reached case by case.[25] Publicizing a draft of the League plan would serve no useful purpose and would definitely stir up opposition. Some would feel the plan too radical and complicated; others would criticize it as too conservative and simple. Above all, publication of a definite charter would invite criticism by senators "of the Lodge type."[26]

Wilson's hand was forced by the middle of 1918 by a rapidly growing public demand for a definite charter of peace. House, who since 1917 had headed a committee to analyze public and official opinion on a league both in the United States and abroad, was commissioned, July 8, to draft a league plan. A few days later he brought the President a long, detailed, and complicated charter. There was much in it with which Wilson might have quarreled, but he shortened it by only a few lines and made only two major changes in its substance: the first was to drop the international court; the second was to strengthen the enforcement of guarantees. Wilson added a provision for "any military force that may be needed. . ." to House's guarantee of moral force and economic boycott.[27] The pledge of the Pan-American Pact was thus essentially repeated. The President did not, however, reintroduce the guarantee of a republican form of government to member states, for none of the prospective members of the League of Nations were autocracies.

This was Wilson's only draft of the League up to the time he went to the peace conference. The covenant still remained in Wilson's view a matter of spirit rather than law. The President, said Sir William Wiseman who was closely associated with him at the time, believes that there must be a league and that it must be virile.[28] Details did not concern him. So matters rested in the fateful fall of 1918.

Wilson, said his friend and biographer Ray Stannard Baker, was an editor and compiler who did not originate any part of the charter of the League. Though this assertion is literally correct, it does not fairly express Wilson's part in the development of the charter. In selecting from the suggestions of others he gave inordinate emphasis to those theories he believed to be most vital. One of these was that the League must be established as quickly as possible. Another was that peace must be enforced. In fact, most of Wilson's advisors opposed the guarantee of peace in the positive form the President advocated. Almost alone in his conviction, Wilson was largely responsible for insisting that the mutual guarantee be made the heart of the Covenant.

In the all-important matter of gaining Senate approval for his program, Wilson was pessimistic from the beginning. Not inclined toward conciliation, he made no progress in 1917 and 1918 toward achieving a meeting of minds with Senate critics of a league of nations. A political leader keenly aware of the realities confronting him, Wilson must have known, as his advisors kept telling him, that the biggest obstacle to the success of a league was the mutual guarantee. Again and again Wilson was told that the guarantee would never win Senate approval. Yet he refused to abandon or modify his program. How did he hope to see it through?

CHAPTER IV

League Is Tied to the Treaty

As Wilson made preparations in the fall of 1918 for the Peace Conference in Paris, the evident opposition of the Senate and, to a lesser degree, the resistance of the American public to a league of mutual guarantee impressed itself upon him. For good or ill Wilson decided that the League issue had given rise to irreconcilable differences between his position and that of Senate leaders. There was no practical way to compromise the obligation of the mutual guarantee. It was not analogous, for example, to a general appropriations bill where opposing forces might split the difference without wrecking the operations of the government. As long as agreement was feasible and possible a wise President would avoid offending the opposition. If agreement could not be reached, a prudent President would give up the project altogether; a strong President would attempt to overwhelm the opposition.

Wilson determined to persist; in the League lay the only hope of lasting peace. Striving to find some political formula to assure establishment of a league, Wilson decided to make the League the first order of business at the Conference and to tie it inseparably to the preliminary peace treaty. Then critics who attacked the League must risk jeopardizing the peace settlement. Even more important in recommending this plan was Wilson's theory, held until March, 1919, that the preliminary peace treaty with the League attached would constitute an agreement not requiring Senate approval.

When Wilson suggested to House in August that the League and the Treaty be combined, the Colonel objected strongly but unsuccessfully. Lansing was not consulted at all but would have opposed tying the League to the Treaty.

Sometime later when he saw the plan in action, the Secretary of State called it the work of a "foxy ward politician" and attributed the whole scheme to Colonel House. Wilson went ahead with his plan. Although he did not announce it publicly until March, 1919, he declared in his September 27 speech in New York that the constitution of the League of Nations was "in a sense the most important part of the peace settlement itself."

Lansing on the one hand and Hays on the other traced the failure of the League to the rise of partisan spirit in the fall of 1918. Both charged Wilson with instigating it. Historians subsequently have analyzed Wilson's fanning of partisanship into a consuming flame through such decisions as the call for a Democratic Congress and the slight of the Senate in selecting the official delegation. But these decisions were made as the last desperate attempt to claim victory. They were mistakes simply because the strategy failed. There is little reason to suppose that a conciliatory policy would have assured success.

Wilson was not in the fall of 1918, as Lansing and Hays implied, jeopardizing a state of bi-partisan harmony for the sake of a few votes. Only the necessity of winning a war had held in check what was by 1918 an aroused partisanship abetted by a virulent hatred for Wilson as a person, a Democratic leader, and a symbol of Executive dominance. Taft, Roosevelt, Root, and Hays on July 19 and July 20, many weeks before Wilson's appeal, called for the election of a Republican Congress as a necessity in conducting the war. Lodge, speaking as a party leader, attacked the President's peace program in a Senate speech August 23 and in a press statement supported the Taft, Roosevelt, Root, Hays dictum that only a Republican Congress could assure complete victory. Renewing his attack on October 7, Lodge demanded the complete destruction of Germany while dismissing the Fourteen Points as unimportant. Theodore Roosevelt, a few days later, underscored the Senator's demands.

At this point Wilson, taking a step he had long contemplated, called upon voters to return a Democratic Congress.[1] His October appeal was actually the last rather than the first step in his struggle with the Senate. Certainly there was little reason to hope for League support from a Republican-dominated Senate. Lansing, a keen observer of the political scene, described (before the October appeal was made) the existence of a personal hatred for Wilson in the Senate, bitter and strong enough to blot out patriotism. Lodge, Penrose, Wadsworth, and others would stop at nothing in a campaign to discredit the President by denouncing anything and everything he did.[2]

Meanwhile, the struggle over the as yet unborn League continued. Notable amid the Republican attacks on Wilson was the lack of enthusiasm that many Democrats felt for their leader's peace plans. Anti-imperialists of 1898 were still opposed to any policy that threatened the traditional isolationism of the United States. Even among Wilson's official delegation, frequently described as a group of handpicked rubber-stamps, there was almost complete opposition to the mutual guarantee. This opposition became apparent as Wilson, who had done no intensive work on the charter itself from August until he sailed December 4 for Paris, began discussing his plans with his official advisors while on the voyage to Europe. To members of the Inquiry, the large body of advisors and experts, Wilson explained his position on international guarantees. He did not favor an international police force and believed the full program of the League to Enforce Peace was too complex to be worked out in the short time available at one conference. He indicated that there must be coercion back of the peace-keeping organization, probably in the form of agreements and pledges with the added force of boycotts when needed.[3] In the first meeting with his official delegation to the conference, December 8, the President sought no advice as he outlined his ideas on a league. He left no doubt of his determination to enforce peace. Lansing was disturbed to find the President so "set" on a mutual guarantee of territory by united force or economic pressure. A determination, as he expressed it, to "modify this folly" was evident in Lansing's work during the succeeding weeks.[4]

Lansing failed to alter Wilson's plans. But his reasons for opposing the positive mutual guarantee are significant as representative of the frame of mind of many other American intellectuals who were not opposed to Wilson personally and were supporters of his political party. Lansing was, from the time the issue came up in 1916, fundamentally opposed to a guarantee by force which he felt was unnecessary, impractical, and politically undesirable. The guarantee was unnecessary, Lansing believed, as enforcement would not be a problem of the new league for peace. Universalization of democracy would follow the defeat of the Central Powers. In the new age of democracy the people could make their voices heard in the councils of state. The people hated war; there would be no more war. The people hated deception; there would be no more broken treaties. Consequently in a league composed only of democratic states, subject to the will of peace-loving people who believed in honoring all international commitments, there would be no breaking of the peace and no need to suppress lawlessness by military force.

That collective coercion was unnecessary in a world organization was fortunate, thought Lansing, for while the theory of enforcing peace seemed sound, the mechanical difficulties impeding its practical application were insurmountable. Enforcement of peace by an international army would be impossible. There could never be any world patriotism to support a super-national organization, and an international force, for this reason, would inevitably be inferior to any national army. Furthermore, any attempt at enforcement by the international organization, Lansing maintained, must run counter to the national interest of at least one of its members. Unless the offending state was very small, the international organization must suffer defeat.[5]

Besides rejecting the principle of international force as impractical in application, Lansing believed that advocating an affirmative guarantee was nothing short of political dynamite—sure to incite unending troubles both at home and abroad.[6] With remarkable accuracy he foresaw in 1918 the major trials that would beset Article Ten in 1919. The Senate, Lansing was convinced, would not accept the affirmative guarantee. It was of doubtful constitutionality and a definite threat to the senatorial prerogative to declare war. Even if the guarantee should be adopted, the Senate would demand the right to give specific authorization for each instance in which sanctions were used. The use of force on an international scale was a drastic break with American tradition, and neither the Senate nor the public was convinced that traditions must be sacrificed.

As a constructive critic, Lansing suggested an alternative to Wilson's positive guarantee. The nations, under a plan Lansing had developed as early as 1916, would accept a negative guarantee—a pledge not to commit aggression themselves.[8] At the same time no responsibility would be assumed for the conduct of any other nation.

While Lansing was reading accurately the future of Article Ten, the Senate opposition to a revolution in American foreign policy was, like the President, laying the foundations for a campaign. They clearly saw the outline of Wilson's strategy in calling for immediate action and combining the League with the Treaty.

Albert J. Beveridge, no longer a senator but still very much a politician and an influential one by reason of his writing, his oratory, and his personal correspondence with Republican leaders, urged a policy of delay in response to Wilson's demand for immediate action. Beveridge, once an ardent imperialist, explained the seeming incongruity of his opposition to Wilson's large policy. Expansion advanced the national interests; an international organization to promote peace did not. Describing himself as "an American Nationalist with a big N," he wrote in 1918: "How amazing that these gentlemen should wish to denature the American Republic . . . without any real discussion or debate of it." Long debates preceded the adoption of the Declaration of Independence and the Constitution. Certainly so fundamental a change in American foreign policy as membership in a league should require equally long consultation. Policies that might destroy the Monroe Doctrine and nullify American traditions in foreign policy should not be accepted lightly.[9]

Lodge and Knox attacked the combining of the League and the Treaty even before Wilson publicly announced his plan. In a memorandum on December 2 to Republican peace commissioner Henry White, Lodge warned that the proposed League must "under no circumstances" be made a part of the peace treaty. Any attempt to combine the two instruments would lead to long delay and make adoption of an unamended treaty by the Senate "extremely doubtful."[10] The next day Knox introduced a resolution calling for a separate peace treaty to be negotiated at once while formulation of the League was postponed until "some future time." Knox protested in a Senate speech, December 18, any undue haste in considering the League of Nations. In his speech he made use of some of Beveridge's letters to him on the subject. Lodge, after a conference with Roosevelt, publicly warned the Allies not to include the League in the Treaty. Any provisions not relating directly to peace could not be forced through the Senate. The Senate, Lodge warned, was not adverse to rejecting treaties entirely or amending them drastically.[12]

The opposition of such prominent leaders in government and the assertion by Republican leaders late in November that Wilson by his failure in the 1918 election had forfeited his authority to speak for the American people apparently confirmed the President's judgment that he must force his program through. Upon reaching Paris he announced that the foundation of a League of Nations must be the first and foremost task of the conference. This he found almost immediately was not the wish of European statesmen. For a time it appeared that the division of conquered territory would be the first order of business, but Wilson eventually succeeded in securing the appointment of a commission to draft a constitution for a league. With Wilson as chairman, the commission began its sessions February 3, meeting at night so as not to delay work of the conference.

Meanwhile, the American contingent to the conference was hard at work preparing a final draft of a league to present to the commission when it met.

The work was complicated by fundamental disagreement over the nature of the mutual guarantee. Lansing, after failing in his first attempt to persuade Wilson to accept a negative guarantee, sought, during late December, to enlist the support of the other members of the official delegation. With White and Bliss he succeeded, but House, Lansing complained, could not tell the difference between a positive and a negative guarantee.[13] On December 23 he again sent a draft of his negative guarantee to Wilson. There was no reply, but Lansing continued to work for the adoption of his plan. He thought by January 7 that House was "entirely converted" to the negative guarantee.[14] It was supported by two other of Wilson's aides, David Hunter Miller and Gordon Auchincloss, in their critical memorandum prepared for Wilson on his first draft of the covenant. Calling attention to the dangers of a positive guarantee, they proposed, in almost the exact language used by Lansing, a negative guarantee.[15] The legal staff on January 6, probably at House's insistence, incorporated the negative guarantee into a draft of the covenant.

The trend toward Lansing's plan came to a halt the next day when Wilson read the proposal for a negative guarantee. He rejected it at once as too weak; an affirmative guarantee was absolutely necessary to the prevention of war.[16] On January 10 this decision was made final when Wilson met with his official commission to discuss the League. Lansing, in a last effort to block the adoption of the positive guarantee, during a somewhat stormy meeting urged that the entire draft be abandoned and a new start made. Wilson, although he had invited suggestions, was not disposed to accept them and seemed more interested in approval for his own ideas than in proposals for their improvement. Lansing was now convinced that his negative guarantee would be rejected. In deep discouragement over what he felt was a major blunder, he considered resigning from the delegation.[17]

Instead of resigning Lansing continued to work against the immediate adoption of the American draft. As a substitute he proposed seeking agreement on broad general principles rather than attempting to incorporate in the preliminary treaty a complete constitution for a league. There was much, he felt, to recommend such a course. Delaying final drafting of the League Covenant would afford added opportunity to modify provisions as public reaction might dictate. Moreover, it was inadvisable, if not impossible, in the month that remained before Wilson's scheduled return to the United States to attempt so ambitious a task as drafting a final constitution of the League.

Once again Wilson rejected Lansing's advice. It did not

meet the political problem of forcing a League on a reluctant Senate. Wilson was correct, even Lansing agreed, in assuming that "the only way to obtain his plan for a League was to insist upon its practical acceptance before peace was negotiated, and that, unless he took advantage of the universal demand for peace by making the acceptance of the Covenant a condition precedent, he would be unable to obtain its adoption."

Lansing failed to delete the positive guarantee from the American version of the Covenant either directly or by delay. Wilson on his own responsibility had made a fateful decision. No other member of his inner circle on the official delegation and few of his advisors on the commission favored the positive mutual guarantee. Nevertheless, House and Miller, after the January 10 meeting with Wilson, incorporated the positive guarantee into the official American covenant. When this version was combined with the British plan in the Hurst-Miller draft, the positive guarantee despite British reluctance was made a part of the draft presented for discussion to the League of Nations Commission at its first meeting.[18] Wilson had driven his fundamental idea through against strong opposition.

This fourth and last draft of what was to become Article Ten differed in one important respect from the first three. They had contained a long statement providing for such territorial readjustments in the future "as may in the judgment of three fourths of the Delegates be demanded by the welfare and manifest interest of the peoples concerned. . . ." These changes were to be made upon the principle that "the peace of the world is superior in importance to every question of political jurisdiction or boundary." Wilson recognized that there was a delicate balance to be established in protecting the status quo while providing for the inevitable changes that time would impose. Nevertheless, to him the guarantee of the status quo was of paramount importance. At last he decided that this guarantee would be weakened by being included in the same article with the provision guaranteeing peaceful change in territorial boundaries.[19] In reaching this decision he may have been prompted by British insistence on protecting the status quo.[20] At any event, in the draft put before the League commission, the provision for territorial change was transferred from what became Article Ten of the final draft to Article Nineteen. Unfortunately the provision for change in Article Nineteen was ignored, while the freezing of the status quo in the revised Article Ten was singled out by senators as a major point of attack. It was charged that the League, because of the rigidity of Article Ten, was nothing more than an instrument to assure the victors the spoils of war.

During the ten days of discussion on the Covenant by the League Commission, the most serious debate arose over the matter of enforcing the decrees of the proposed League. France demanded an international army, or at the very least, an international general staff—in essence the continuation of the anti-German alliance. Wilson was opposed. The American Constitution would not permit the limitation on sovereignty required by an international army. During the heated debate, the British sided with the United States. At length, plans for an international army were abandoned.[21] Article Ten was not strengthened. In fact it was somewhat weakened in deference to British reluctance to accept responsibility for a territorial guarantee. Wilson's original statement that the Powers would "unite in guaranteeing to each other political independence and territorial integrity" was modified to read that the Powers "undertake to respect and preserve as against external aggression the territorial integrity and existing political independence of all Members of the League." The original statement was changed also to correct a flaw in the earlier drafts, the failure to devise a method for executing the guarantee. The final draft provided for the League Council to "advise upon the means by which these obligations shall be fulfilled."[22]

Still, the actual method of enforcement was not clear. Wilson never contemplated, as his opponents so frequently charged, the establishment of an international army. Even the theory of a league based on the executive authority of the Major Powers was unsatisfactory to him, for he rejected such proposals from House, Cecil, and Clemenceau. These were, Wilson insisted, but reincarnations of the old and unholy diplomatic system of Europe. Nor did he favor compulsory arbitration. Possibly he did not have at the time any definite positive plan for enforcement but hoped when his general design was accepted that these vital details would fall into place.

The supreme duty of the Conference, in Wilson's view, was creating a league, an undertaking not to be compared with the routine task of making a peace treaty. By the creation of a league, Wilson told House, "the world was being turned upside down and a new order was being inaugurated." The Treaty was "merely the question of boundaries and what not; which had been the subject matter of peace conferences since time immemorial." House agreed that Wilson could "change the order of things throughout the world."

In accordance with his plan, the President had been working to this point to include the League in the preliminary treaty ending the war and renewing commercial intercourse. He was still under the mistaken impression that the preliminary treaty including the League could be brought into force by the act of the Executive without ratification by the Senate. When Wilson left for the United States in February, he felt the success of his project was already assured. He had the League, and he had met the popular demand for the immediate restoration of peace. The Senate was powerless, so he thought, to block his path and the statesmen of Europe could now devote all the time they wished to the routine task of making a definitive peace treaty dealing with boundaries and claims.

In this mood there is little wonder that Wilson was not anxious to attempt to placate the Senate. But at the insistence of House, Wilson finally agreed to invite the Senate and House committees on foreign relations to a dinner at the White House. But he requested in his invitation that no debate on the League take place prior to the meeting.[23]

In this hope he was disappointed. The constitution of the Covenant which he had kept from view for so long was now public property. Senators did not wait for Presidential explanations but began their criticism within twenty-four hours after the publication of the Covenant. Republicans Poindexter and Borah led the attack. Poindexter called the League the most entangling and permanent alliance conceivable, one that would force the United States "to participate in the wars and controversies of every other nation." Borah castigated the Covenant as the greatest triumph of English diplomacy in three centuries. Democratic Senator Reed joined the chorus and declared that the size of America's military forces under the League would be controlled by "the gracious permission of eight gentlemen, six of whom probably cannot speak our language." These negative attacks overshadowed Senator Hamilton J. Lewis's defense of Article Ten as a deterrent to most wars. Senator Cummins challenged Lewis with the opinion that Article Ten prohibited desirable change and that "nothing could surpass it in repugnance to good morals and to the civilization of the world."[24]

Meanwhile, Wilson had landed in Boston and delivered a speech in which he declared that his fighting blood was stirred. The Senate's blood was already up. Under these circumstances the previously scheduled White House dinner to placate the Senate took place under most inauspicious conditions. The critics of the President's program were intent on finding faults. Lodge was not too engrossed in international affairs to note that Mrs. Wilson's fingernails were unkept. Brandegee found the dinner very bad, regretting that there was nothing to drink and that the cigars were poor. He was further irritated when Wilson lined the congressmen up in rows like a class and announced that he had no statement to make but would answer questions. Brandegee had anticipated that Wilson would go over the Covenant article by article and was surprised that the President did not even bring a copy.[25] Wilson got many more questions than he had expected. His critics complained that his answers revealed nothing but his ignorance as to the meaning and effect of the Covenant. The President's friends denied all this and praised his exposition of the League. But both friend and foe agreed the meeting failed utterly to bring the President and the Senate closer to agreement on a program for peace.

Possibly the most important result of the meeting was Wilson's assertion that the Covenant would not be much amended; it would be too difficult to gain the agreement of the other signatories. This policy afforded enemies of the League the possibility of a plausible but pernicious strategy of amending the League to extinction. The President was so discouraged by the results of the White House dinner meeting that he upbraided House for having suggested it in the first place.[26]

This inauspicious bid for good will was, however, only one of a series of evil omens that greeted Wilson's brief peace argosy at home. The Senate debate continued. Lodge counseled the Senate to give much time and thought to investigating all of the implications of League membership. At the same time, he condemned as absurd the idea that a world constitution for peace could be drafted in a few weeks despite the tensions inspired by a war not yet officially ended. The same day Senator Lenroot helped initiate a very important step in the campaign against the League by calling for amendments to the Covenant and demanding that Article Ten be altered to give the Council nothing more than advisory power. Knox and Sherman on March 1 saw great danger in the mutual guarantee. It would be the end of American sovereignty and "the death knell of the American Republic."

Though the tide of debate was much against Wilson, he had some defenders. One of these was Senator Porter J. McCumber, a Republican, who defended Article Ten as the foundation stone for the structure of a league. It was impossible, he declared, to make a clearer or more concise declaration of an agreement to preserve peace.[27] As yet the exact attitude of the Senate on the Covenant was so indefinite as to be a matter of conjecture.

Unfortunately for Wilson the danger for opposition senators in failing to consolidate and announce their position was pointed out to Brandegee by a correspondent. This unknown (Brandegee could not recall his name the next day) argued that unless Congress took a definite action disavowing Wilson's program, silence would be interpreted as consent. The President could with assurance and authority return to Paris saying that he represented the will of the American people and their Congress. Brandegee grasped at once the logic of this argument and presented it to Lodge. The latter was afraid that a resolution pledging the Senate to reject the Covenant, while most desirable, could not command a majority. Brandegee contended the resolution need not pass. The same purpose could be served by reading the resolution into the *Record* if as many as one-third of the Senate, enough to defeat the League, opposed it. Lodge agreed and later in the day the two met with Knox to work out a draft. They agreed that no announcement would be made unless the necessary one-third of the Senate signed the resolution. On the next day, Brandegee within an hour got twenty-five signatures. When this became cloakroom knowledge, senators came rushing in to sign and the needed twelve names were soon added.[28]

The resolution, brought up the night of March 13 in the last hours of the session, failed to pass, but it was read into the *Record* with the names of thirty-seven Republicans attached. The number, of course, was more than the necessary one-third of the Senate to veto a treaty and the following day two more names were added. This Republican Round Robin reaffirmed the senators' "sincere desire that the nations of the world should unite to promote peace," to establish a league, and to provide for disarmament. The Senate, however, rejected the League "in the form now proposed" and demanded that the League be separated from the peace treaty.[29]

Wilson suffered a shattering blow. By disavowing his work the Round Robin weakened his influence at the peace table in working to obtain the very amendments it demanded. The President's hope for immediate, uncritical acceptance of a completed league was crushed; his plan to ride the League through the Senate on the coattails of the Treaty was seriously challenged. There was much truth in the *New York Sun's* comment that the League died in the Senate on the night of March 3.[30] The special session of Congress, necessitated by a filibuster on appropriations, was an additional blow, for it afforded Republican opponents of the League greater opportunity to make the *Sun's* words come true. Republicans were now able to organize the Senate with their majority, won in the fateful election of 1918, six months earlier than would otherwise have been the case. Capitol Hill could now become a public forum in which to criticize the President's peace program.[31]

The hostility of Republican senators was not in itself surprising to Wilson, who had only faint hope that the Senate would cooperate willingly with him in launching a revolution in American foreign policy. It must have been a blow, however, to return to the grueling work of the conference realizing that both phases of his plan to cower Senate opposition by presenting a final draft of the League and incorporating it into the peace treaty had been officially and publicly vetoed by the Senate. Nevertheless, he held to his original plan; it was too late to turn back. In a fighting speech in New York just before sailing for Paris, Wilson further dissipated any remaining chance for conciliation with the Senate by defiantly defending his draft of the League and specifically rejecting suggestions that it be separated from the peace treaty, at the same time promising, in reaffirmation of his position taken months before, to tie the Covenant to the Treaty by so many threads "that you cannot dissect the covenant from the treaty without destroying the whole vital structure."[32]

Wilson was still clinging to his original strategy, and the necessity for force seemed vindicated by the reception the Senate had tendered him. But the omnibus strategy was challenged in Paris. During his absence, the President found, the League had been shunted to the background in favor of quick completion of a preliminary treaty restoring a legal state of peace. The Senate, Wilson saw, might willingly accept the preliminary agreement and with peace restored find far less opprobrium in rejecting the League and the final treaty. Moving boldly, Wilson met this threat by simply declaring that the January 25 decision of the Conference to make the League an integral part of the Treaty was "of final force."[33]

More important by far was Wilson's discovery of an even more serious flaw in his strategy. Apparently he hoped, and certainly House had prepared the way,[34] to include the completed Covenant in a preliminary treaty of peace, the terms of which would be repeated in a definitive treaty. During a meeting of the Supreme Council on March 17, 1919, Wilson reflected his views on the matter in the statement that he "had assumed that this preliminary Convention would only be temporary until the complete Treaty was prepared" with its terms restated in the formal treaty. If his understanding was correct, Wilson added, it would not be necessary to submit the preliminary convention to the

Senate. Being uncertain about the matter, the President stated
that he would seek legal advice. At the same meeting Lord
Balfour agreed with Wilson's view that "each clause" of the
preliminary peace would become a part of the final treaty
and that Senate confirmation was not necessary. Should the
Senate have to approve the preliminary convention, added
Balfour, the inevitable delay would render the hope of quick
preliminary settlement nugatory.[35]

Lansing, when questioned on the legal status of the preliminary treaty, March 19, told Wilson that under whatever
name, "exalted Armistice," "agreement," "protocol," or
"modus," it would be a treaty requiring Senate approval.
So perturbed was Wilson by this ruling that he would not
accept it and asked for confirmation from other legal authori-
ties, who, as it developed, supported Lansing.

Wilson was upset, Lansing charged, because he had hoped
to get the Covenant adopted as part of a preliminary
treaty that would respond to the popular demand for an
immediate peace and at the same time "checkmate the opponents of the Covenant in the Senate" by having the League
functioning before the Senate voted on it in the definitive
treaty. "All this was to be done," said Lansing, "without
going through the American constitutional process. . . ."[36]
Lansing may not have been fair. After all, he had been responsible in December, 1916, for the rumor (later denied)
that Wilson hoped to launch his revolution in foreign policy as
Monroe had launched his Doctrine, by a proclamation
requiring no Senate action.[37] The Secretary of State was
unhappy with his secondary role at Paris, was skeptical of
the Covenant, and found it difficult to put his chief's actions
in a favorable light.

Yet there might have been more than an element of truth
in Lansing's charge that the President sought to circumvent
the Senate by placing the Covenant in an executive agreement. Certainly Wilson had made no effort to placate
Senate opposition up to this time and from the start of the
Conference he had planned combining the peace agreements
and the Covenant as closely as possible. Late in February,
House suggested to Wilson by cable that the League of
Nations start functioning at once.[38] The President, March 4,
vetoed the plan, but for reasons of strategy rather than

canons of constitutional law. His critics would gain by exposing so open an attempt "to forestall action by the Senate and commit the country in some practical way from which it would be impossible to withdraw."[39] If the Covenant could be made a part of an executive agreement in line with constitutional practice and accepted as part of a treaty adopted by all members of the Conference, there could be little ground for valid criticism.

After his discovery of the constitutional nature of the preliminary agreement Wilson did lose interest in it. Lansing predicted, with great accuracy, that there would be no preliminary treaty within ten days. Although he made no formal statement, Wilson abandoned the preliminary treaty plan he had previously sponsored and insisted on the questionable procedure of combining into one master treaty the three separate and diverse tasks of drafting a league, restoring peace, and settling the general claims growing out of the war. This procedure, nevertheless, was his best hope for steering the League past its hostile critics at home.

Discovery of the true nature of a preliminary agreement, and the certain knowledge that the League must face judgment by a hostile Senate may well account, also, for Wilson's reluctant yielding in late March to the insistent demands of his advisors for Covenant reservations. Only under extreme provocation would he have undertaken the personally humiliating and difficult task of amending the Covenant. Each American demand would elicit counter demands. The delicate balance of agreement reached in the original draft of the League might be lost. Yet the liberal Republicans, represented by Taft, strongly urged amendments and the Senate Democrats, represented by Hitchcock, pressed them too. Wilson entertained no hope that amendments would convert the Senate opposition. Any change that was suggested to placate the Senate, Wilson rejected.[40] The President's goal now was to win overwhelming public approval for the League, approval so strong that he could force the Covenant down the throat of a protesting Senate. But amendments were imperative if the public was to be won. His advisors argued, too, that minor changes would accomplish major results. Wilson reluctantly agreed to seek amendments. During the next month he labored to incorporate the four most frequently suggested amendments into the Covenant.

The most urgently demanded changes called for assurance of the right to withdraw from the League, exemptions of domestic disputes from the purview of the League, no imposition of mandates on unwilling nations, and specific exclusion of the Monroe Doctrine from the jurisdiction of the League.[41]

Article Ten was not directly attacked in the general demand for amendments even though Hughes demanded its elimination and Root proposed that it be limited to a period of five years. The Article, however, was affected vitally by the proposed reservation to the Monroe Doctrine. If the Doctrine was to be specifically excluded from the force of the Covenant, intervention in the Western Hemisphere by Europeans to execute the mutual guarantee of Article Ten would be impossible. Wilson was so fully aware of the relationship that he at first attached the amendment protecting the Monroe Doctrine to Article Ten.[42] Later it was moved to Article Twenty-one. Wilson argued that the Doctrine could merge in the larger plan for world peace. Nevertheless, a great many Americans (and not all of them blinded by partisanship or personal rancor) could not agree with the President's thesis that Article Ten was a practical and logical extension of the Doctrine to the world. They demanded that the Doctrine be left inviolate. This could not be done without seriously compromising Article Ten.[43]

Thus the letter of liberal Republican demands for reservations to the Covenant was met. At the same time, Wilson's great effort brought him no closer to the real Republican opposition. Henry White attempted to bridge the gap between Wilson on the one hand and Lodge on the other by asking the Senator early in March for a list of amendments necessary to make the Covenant acceptable to the Senate. Root thwarted this attempt at reconciliation. A short time later he countered White's suggestion by sending, without his reasons for supporting them, a list of six proposed amendments. The busy Wilson turned these over to his staff. Miller found some of the suggestions similar to Taft's and the rest of no practical value. In this view Robert Cecil concurred.[44] No effort, however, was made by Wilson or his advisors to mend political fences by indicating that Root's advice had been seriously considered. After all, Wilson sponsored reservations to win public support. He did not hope to persuade the political opposition to accept his plans. Taft and Hitchcock cabled that he had achieved a great success assuring the acceptance of the Covenant. A bulletin from the League to Enforce Peace reported that the amended League had the support of sixty-four senators with only twelve opposed.[45]

Such information confirmed Wilson's own opinion that no further changes were needed. The Covenant as it stood was entirely satisfactory. The people had a blind faith in the League idea that would void further quibbling over detail. But in taking this counsel of perfection and ignoring Root's proposals for change, Wilson left open the avenue his opponents followed so successfully. Their task was to shake public faith in the Covenant. Now that some amendments had been added it could be argued that new and stronger ones were needed. New flaws could be revealed from time to time that required additional safeguards. Most productive of honest doubts were the Root and Hughes amendments limiting or completely nullifying Article Ten.

CHAPTER V

Republicans Demand
Reservations

THE second phase of the revolution of 1919 in American foreign policy was the attempt to agree on minimum amendments. It began with Wilson's return to Paris in March and his successful effort, lasting until late April, to incorporate in the Covenant those amendments most urgently demanded. During this time Henry White of the peace delegation attempted without success to secure from Lodge a list of amendments which the Senate considered necessary. His gesture did elicit an official statement of Republican policy written by Elihu Root and demanding more radical changes than those previously suggested, including limiting the life of Article Ten to five years. Thus, before Wilson finished getting the minimum modifications critics were already demanding more. When he did complete his work, however, it was with the announcement that he could approve no further modifications.

Had the conservatives accepted this work, agreement might have ensued, but they found the obligations of Article Ten still too sharp a break with American traditions. Again calling on Root as a spokesman they demanded, June 21, that Article Ten be eliminated entirely, denounced Wilson's amendments as wholly inadequate, and proposed reservations to correct the flaws. Wilson felt that the whole purpose of the revolution in foreign policy would be sacrificed if Article Ten was lost. Both sides stood firm and the revolution then entered its third and last stage—a struggle for complete victory in which both factions refused to compromise on Article Ten.

The first step toward compromise came on March 9. The only Republican member of the official peace delegation, Henry White, in a personal message asked Lodge for a specific list of changes that would make the Covenant acceptable to the Senate.[1]

Throughout the conference White kept Lodge and Root well informed as to the proceedings through frequent letters of fifteen or twenty typed pages. While not in agreement with all that Wilson did, White was sensitive to the problems of the conference and gave an objective account of the difficulties the President faced in working for a fair settlement. He even went so far as to tell Lodge that his arguments against the treaty, as printed in the newspapers, were inaccurate and misleading.[2] White's opinions, however, carried little weight with either Lodge or Root. After all, he was out of touch with the political situation in the United States. In appealing for amendments they believed White acted, probably unintentionally, as the tool of Wilson.

White, anticipating suspicion, assured Lodge, in an explanatory note, that Wilson did not know of the cabled request for amendments. Lodge at first accepted this explanation and considered a reply. But before doing so he consulted Senator Brandegee, an irreconcilable opponent of any league, who was horrified by White's proposal and implored Lodge not to answer. Fearing that Lodge might do so anyway, Brandegee got Chandler Anderson, a close friend of Lodge and Root, to attempt to get the two together before any reply was made. Anderson succeeded, after soothing Root's anger at not being consulted directly and immediately by his close friend Lodge.[3]

Root advised Lodge to reject White's request. It must, in reality, be Wilson's work. If not inspired by him, it still could not have gotten through the censors in Paris and into the State Department code without the President's knowledge and approval. Aside from Wilson and politics, Root argued that it was unconstitutional as well as degrading to the Senate for its opinions as a body to be transmitted to the President by one of his subordinates, such as White. Root did not believe Wilson was sincerely interested in finding out the ideas of the Senate. He had not sought the Senate's opinions when the body was in session during his February visit. Conditions, it could be argued, had changed so much since the Senate adjourned in March that the President needed information. If so, the proper course was for the President to meet the

Senate in special session. In any event it was improper for
Lodge on his own authority to represent the Senate in suggesting amendments that would commit it. This letter Lodge
sent to White without altering a word.[4] The real purpose of
what he called Wilson's gesture, Root concluded in another
letter to Lodge, was political. "The net is spread in plain sight
of the bird and you are the bird."[5]

This "trap" was avoided, but Republican leaders soon saw
another. In the Senate, Republicans as a party so far had
limited themselves to destructive criticism of the Covenant.
Wilson might yet gain a measure of the political advantage
he sought if it became known that Republicans refused flatly
a specific request to suggest improvements in the unfinished
Covenant. Henry Stimson, after conference with Republican
National Chairman Will H. Hays, decided to seek the political advantages of offering constructive criticism, without
in any way committing the Senate to accept Wilson's program, by having Root draft a list of needed amendments
to be published and sent to Wilson. Root's statement would
improve the political position of the Republican party by
showing its constructive interest in the League and would
unify the Republican factions by setting a policy toward
the League agreeable to both radicals and conservatives.[6]
An additional purpose, according to Will Hays, was to clarify
the public mind by affording "the best possible interpretation" of the League, and to keep the peacemaking "as far
as possible out of politics."[7] Truly it would take a remarkable *tour de force* to meet all of these varied ends.

But Root was a remarkable man. With great dignity and
no hint at the elaborate preparation that had gone before,
Root, ostensibly in response to a letter from Hays, wrote
with "subtle brain and a cunning hand" a seven-thousand-
word letter explaining the changes needed in the League
Covenant.[8] Subsequently cabled to Paris, the message was
put before Wilson and endorsed by White, an official member of the peace delegation. Root's educational document, as
Hays promised, was mailed to one million individuals and
reached ten million readers through five thousand newspapers.[9]

The letter suggested six amendments. First, Root demanded that the whole League be based on the theory of

obligatory arbitration of justiciable disputes. There should be periodic conferences to develop international law and increase its effectiveness. Second, to protect the Monroe Doctrine, he recommended that the United States agree to aid Europe but reject European aid in the Western Hemisphere. Third, the United States should be the sole authority in domestic matters. Fourth, a commission should be formed to inspect the progress of disarmament. Fifth, there must be provision for a conference to revise the entire League some years in the future after the passions of war had cooled. Sixth, the life of Article Ten with its provision to "respect and preserve . . . existing political independence" should be limited to five years. The League, modified according to the six amendments, said Root in conclusion, ought to be adopted by the United States.

As to the all-important issue of Article Ten, Root's first impulse had been to eliminate it. Root never accepted the idea that one generation must undertake to guarantee by an inflexible pledge the territorial status quo for all future generations. At the same time, unsettled conditions in Europe made it imperative that the League have the authority of Article Ten until the restoration of real peace. The United States "could not quit" while there remained a responsibility to discharge. Consequently, in a compromise with himself, Root drew the amendment limiting the application of Article Ten to a five-year period—the only approval he ever gave the Article.[10]

The six proposals, possibly by coincidence, included three that Wilson had already rejected several times. While sincere students of international affairs might feel they were necessary, earnest advocates of honest compromise must have recognized them, even at this time, as stumbling blocks to agreement. For example, Wilson had never accepted the theory of compulsory arbitration. Certainly Wilson would not favor rewriting the Covenant in the near future. Above all, he would brook no alteration in the text of Article Ten. Whether designed to do so or not, Root's letter put Wilson at a disadvantage, for it was virtually certain he would not seek all of the changes. Consequently, the charge could be made that Wilson was partisan, uncooperative, and stubborn.

White's effort to bridge the gap between President and Senate demonstrated the tremendous influence over American policy exerted by Root, a private citizen at that time. Throughout the remainder of the Senate debate on the League, Root had more to do than any other person with choosing the policy followed by Republican senators and drafting reservations on which they could act in unity.

Root's significance in the debate on the League of Nations lay in the weight his opinion carried. His government service as former Secretary of War, Secretary of State, and Senator had made him well known to the American people and so respected that there was a veritable "Root cult." Socially, as well as politically, he was an associate of Lodge, Taft, Hughes, Roosevelt, Brandegee, White, Scott, Anderson, Lowell, Lansing, and many other influential leaders. In close personal contact with most of them during the period of the League debate, he was the elder statesman of the Republican party, the personal confidant of its leaders in 1919, and the attorney for the Senate. Both the people of the nation as a whole and the Republican party would more readily respond to the judgment of Root than of any other American of the time.

As to Article Ten, the heart of the League Covenant, Root sincerely and consistently opposed it. He had never favored the principle of a political international organization based on a commitment to enforce peace. Root would not support the Taft Arbitration Treaties of 1911 because he believed their promise of action to maintain peace could not be executed. In his Nobel Prize address, which was to have been delivered September 8, 1914, he described an international police force with power to enforce right conduct as an "attractive idea" but nothing more than "the counsel of perfection."[11] For the same reason he never associated himself with the League to Enforce Peace although offered the vice-presidency of the organization. Root believed that attempts "to maintain a fixed and immutable relation of territory and opportunity among the nations" must always fall before the forces working for change. It was natural, he conceded, for democracies to think in terms of an international law as binding upon the governments of the world. Respect for law was the essential condition for the existence of democracies. But they tended to forget that the effectiveness of law in a democracy rested not on physical force but on the will of the people to accept and observe the law. Hence, Root could have little faith in or sympathy for plans to guarantee territorial integrity by military force.[12]

His position he made clear again in 1918 in response to a letter from House. In the distant future Root could visualize a community of nations recognizing a breach of the peace as the concern of all and coercing aggressors by moral pressure and military force. In the world of 1918, however, there was no community of interests among nations strong enough to make the theory of collective action workable. The American people in 1918 would be unwilling to break with traditions by accepting blanket future commitments to go to war or to attempt to alter events not directly related to national policy.[13] Further, Root believed the Constitution forbade making an agreement including an automatic obligation to go to war; Congressional sanction for war must be given in each specific case. Consequently the cause of world peace would be hindered rather than advanced if the United States made agreements which it was not prepared to honor.[14]

Characteristic of Root's work was the fact that what amounted to a flat denial of Wilson's league was interpreted by some as an agreement in principle. House, after showing the letter to Wilson, wrote to Root: "I do not believe there will be much difficulty in bringing our minds in harmony upon some such plan."[15] Such optimism was not justified. Root believed the mutual guarantee Wilson wanted was entirely impractical. On this issue, subsequently brought to debate in Article Ten, Root and Wilson were completely irreconcilable.[16] Wilson soon realized this fact and described Root as a "hopeless reactionary." Certainly Root was in sincere and fundamental opposition to the principle of Article Ten at all times during the debate on the League. There must be no outside "control over national independence of action."[17]

Root's objections to the League, however, were not limited to his clear and consistent opposition to its fundamental tenets. In private he sharply disapproved Wilson's whole conduct of the peace negotiations. For the President to go to Paris in person was, Root believed, a violation of the Constitution. A President could not leave

the continental limits of the United States and retain the
authority of office. Aside from that, it was a grave
mistake for so bungling a diplomat as Wilson to interject
himself into the situation. In doing so he had made
himself the chief obstacle to a successful league. His "bully-
ing and opinionated and tactless methods" were a "national
calamity" costing the United States much good will in
both France and England.[18] Furthermore, Wilson by
going to Paris and taking Lansing with him had complicated
matters by removing the normal and necessary check that a
President and Secretary of State could exercise over the work
of subordinate negotiators. Wilson forced the Senate to assume the duty of reviewing his work at the Conference, a
task the Senate discharged, Root felt, "with great assiduity
and manifest sincerity of purpose and public spirit."[19] Wilson
deprecated this service and with ruthless defiance deliberately disregarded the Senate's traditional rights and duties.
As a result, senators "were boiling over with a perfectly
natural rage because of Wilson's refusal to consult them and
his practical denial of their right to discuss the subject at all.
The offensively arrogant way in which the subject was
presented . . . produced a very disagreeable effect. . . ." To
Wilson a critic of the League was an opponent, and "anyone
who does not swallow the agreement whole is opposed to
peace."[20] Thus, Wilson, in Root's opinion, was seeking to
introduce a new foreign policy, a major break with the
past, by methods that denied the Senate its constitutional
duty to advise and consent.

Withal, Root was an intensely devoted member of the
Republican party.[21] His statesmanship was not of such an
exalted character as to let him forget the approaching 1920
presidential election and the Republican losses in 1912 and
1916 to Wilson. He recognized, aside from any personal
convictions, that the paramount political consideration was
to develop a league policy that would command the loyalty
of all Republicans. In his view he had the concurrence of
Roosevelt. In mid-December 1918 the dying ex-President
counseled Root and Lodge to evolve a program of amendments designed to alter the League drastically while pro-
fessing publicly complete loyalty to the ideal of a Covenant.[22]

As Root sincerely opposed the League, no problem of

reconciling ideals with realities plagued him. His great concern was to translate Republican sentiment against the League into a constructive program. His consummate skill in drafting political documents acceptable to diametrically opposed factions and the public image of him as a wise friend of the League whose judgment was undistorted by partisan considerations made Root the most formidable representative of the great body of conservative opinion opposing Wilson's revolution in foreign policy.

Root moved to a position of leadership shortly before the final draft of the League was accepted in Paris. The Republican demands as set forth in his March letter Wilson ignored. Article Ten, far from being limited to five years, remained unamended. Wilson cabled Lansing more than a month before the final draft was accepted that there would be no amendment to Article Ten—"the king pin of the whole structure. . . ."[23] The Senate would have to accept the Article or reject the entire treaty and suffer the consequences. Opposition would be overcome by aggressive attack.

When the final draft of the Covenant was published on April 28, Lodge called Root by long distance phone and declared the amendments on the Monroe Doctrine, domestic issues, and Article Ten unsatisfactory. The problem was to gain the concurrence of a majority in the Senate in a demand for additional and stronger amendments. To this end Root's help was "vitally necessary." His position on the issue, said Lodge, would control the votes of Senate Democrats as well as Republicans.[24] Presumably Root assured Lodge of support, although he made no definite move for some weeks. The next day Lodge and Senator Curtis telegraphed all Republican senators to reserve final expression of opinion until the amended draft of the Covenant could be studied and discussed at conferences. In a supplemental press statement Lodge indicated that further amendment would be needed if the Covenant was "to promote peace and not endanger certain rights of the United States. . . ."

In the meantime little could be done until Congress convened for a special session on May 19 and the rest of the Treaty was completed in Paris. Immediately on convening, an impatient Congress demanded to see the Treaty and finally, through the efforts of a Chicago newspaper and Senator

Borah, got the completed but unsigned document on June 9,
nineteen days before it became official. To Root the loud
squabble over obtaining copies of the Treaty was poor politics.
He chided Senator Brandegee, one of the leaders on this
issue, saying that the people were finding in Wilson rather
than in the Senate Republicans the strong leadership they
desired in a time of confusion. If the public became convinced that the Senate was quarreling about trifles, Root
continued, the President's leadership would be enhanced
further. Brandegee, not heeding the warning, challenged
Root "to come out in the *open* with the rest of us." Otherwise, he should leave the fight against the Treaty to those
who were in the midst of the battle in Washington.[25]
Brandegee's challenge and the failure of Knox's June 10
resolution to cut the Treaty and Covenant apart convinced
Root that the time to give his "vitally necessary" help had
come. Going to Washington, he conferred with Lodge, and
with irreconcilables Brandegee and Knox. They agreed that
Root should write a letter to Lodge explaining what further
reservations were essential. The three senators read and approved Root's work before it was published on June 21, still
a week before Germany signed the Treaty.

Again Root's facile pen served many purposes. Hays
could write that this letter, like the earlier one, was drawn
"with no other thought than as a public service to all the
voters of America." But he did not deny that the letter would
also indicate a constructive League policy on which the two
sharply divergent factions of the Republican party could
unite.[26]

In the text of this widely distributed statement, Root
noted Wilson's failure to accept some of the suggested amendments. The revisions he had succeeded in getting relating to
the Monroe Doctrine, domestic disputes, and withdrawal
from the League, were unsatisfactory also. More important
was Wilson's failure to modify Article Ten. Setting aside
previous arguments that the Article was needed for five
years, Root demanded elimination of so inflexible a commitment to a "vague universal obligation." The United States
ought not to accept it, for America could do more for
peace by "keeping out of the petty quarrels that arise than
by binding ourselves to take part in them."[27] Root was not

seeking simply to make political capital of the issue. He was speaking in good conscience, having honestly reached that fortunate state wherein conscience and expediency directed the same course.

No real progress toward ratification of the League of Nations by the Senate, it can be seen in retrospect, was made after Root's historic declaration on June 21, 1919. What additional impetus was needed to unify Republicans was provided by Wilson's reiteration upon the completion of the treaty that amendments must be avoided, as they would lead to futile negotiations and interminable delay. Lodge reported forty-seven senators pledged to support Root's reservation to Article Ten. Most of the major leaders of the Republican party in and out of the Senate, whatever their feelings on the League, were able to unite on the Root program for a league with reservations.

In announcing party policy on July 16, Chairman Will H. Hays declared, "The situation respecting the League Covenant is simply this: There must be *effective reservations*. These reservations must safeguard the sovereignty of the United States in every particular; . . . must either eliminate Article X entirely or so modify it that our own Congress shall be morally as well as legally free after a specific period to decide when and where and to what extent our soldiers shall be employed; . . . .

"It is up to the Administration to decide whether it will or will not accept these essential guarantees of American independence, which would unquestionably be promptly accepted by the other nations."[28]

Root at all times maintained a keen sense of the best political form in which to present Senate objections to the treaty. Reservations, regardless of other considerations, were expedient as political moves. Wilson claimed the League as his own creation; reservations would serve more effectively than amendments to put the stamp of the Senate, and its Republican members in particular, on the Covenant. Amendments under international law, as Root explained to Kellogg, must have the assent of foreign powers to become operative. On the other hand, reservations, contrary to Wilson's argument, did not require the express approval of other signatories to a treaty, although they could raise definite objections.

Foreign nations probably would accept reservations and in so doing approve, in effect, the work of the Senate. Wilson would suffer, for it would appear he could have had the changes the Senate recommended if he had honestly sought them.[29]

The position of the Republican party—the League with reservations—Root emphasized, vindicated the constitutional power of the Senate as opposed to the President's "assertion of unlimited authority" for his office. It was a just and honorable position. Only thus could the Republican opposition to the Treaty be defended as "a great political achievement, and a successful struggle for the maintenance of our system of government," rather than be criticized as a "mere subterfuge for the purpose of defeating by indirection a Treaty which the Senate did not dare defeat directly."[30]

The exact content and form of these reservations was a major problem. Root, "the attorney for the Senate," was in constant touch with Lodge, giving him the benefit of his political sagacity, his knowledge of international law, and his unmatched skill in drafting reservations acceptable to the greatest possible number of Republican senators. Assisting Root was his friend and business associate, Chandler Anderson, who had worked with the legal staff of the American delegation in drafting the Treaty in Paris. Anderson spent the entire month of August in Washington making suggestions for reservations and translating the ideas of others into proper legal form. His work was indispensable to Lodge in his unflagging efforts to get all members of his party in the Senate to agree on the exact intent and wording of each reservation.

In addition to his other work Root, by reason of his vast personal prestige and long experience in government, was able to persuade individual senators to accept particular reservations on a number of occasions.

Reservations to the League changed in number and character during the summer and fall. At first, there had been suggestions for a few general changes, but the reservation-makers in the Senate became increasingly explicit and demanding as the debate continued. Anderson explained, as did Lodge, that the trend toward definiteness developed because the more the Senate learned about the Treaty, the more dangerous it appeared.[31] The clamor for more and stronger reservations pleased Lodge and, to a lesser degree, Root.[32]

As to Article Ten, Root's letters relative to drafting a reservation for it showed him to be sincerely and fundamentally opposed to such a method of preserving peace. He believed the Article would "surrender the moral power of the United States" to uphold justice, "the only sure basis of peace." The Shantung issue, Root thought, offered an excellent example of the sort of injustice the United States must countenance and support by force under Article Ten.[33] Root discounted Wilson's contention that the United States was bound by a moral but not a legal obligation; such an argument was nothing more than an attempt to confuse the issue. Article Ten, Root believed, was a legal pledge to take definite action in certain stipulated circumstances; in short, an alliance and as such a violation of America's traditional policy. The Article's automatic commitments would nullify the Senate's influence in shaping foreign policy. Even more disastrous would be the refusal of the American people to honor the obligation in Article Ten, even if the Article should be accepted by the Senate.[34]

Root, more than any other individual, had made it possible for honest opponents of change to unite the Republican party on the politically expedient program of reservations, and by his direct attacks on Article Ten did much to make it one of the chief targets of the reservationists. There is little evidence that Root moved in statesmanlike oblivion to the practical political advantages of the position he charted. At the same time, it must be said that he was sincere in opposing Article Ten; it was not in keeping with his personal convictions or with the Republican party's traditional policy of judicial settlement of international questions.

According to Root's private correspondence, as well as his public statements, he felt adoption of the League with reservations was necessary not because of its positive virtues but "to bring about speedy peace and set industry in motion again. . . ." At the same time he cautioned that the American people "should not regard this agreement as a real solution of the problem. It is on a false basis, and will not accomplish what is claimed of it." Wilson had sought in the one Treaty of Versailles both to meet a present crisis and to prepare for future peace. The attempt to combine these two conflicting purposes had resulted in the unsatisfactory solution of each of them.[35]

By his opposition to Article Ten, Root caused many intelligent Americans to begin to measure the proposals of the League by the traditional standards of the nation's foreign policy. To his arguments were added, subconsciously at least, the admonitions of the founding fathers. John Quincy Adams had spoken not only for his generation but also for one a century later when he declared in 1823 that the United States should keep itself "free to act as emergencies arise and not tie ourselves down to any principles which might immediately afterwards be brought to bear against ourselves."

An implacable opponent of Article Ten, Root translated his opposition into a practical and plausible political program. The party accepted the program, but some members may have been impelled by expediency rather than agreement with his views on Article Ten. Yet there seems to have been an almost unanimous rejection of the Article by Republican leaders. What, for example, did the titular head of the party, Charles Evans Hughes, say about Article Ten?

No Republican was more consistently opposed to Article Ten than Hughes. The first time he read the Article he declared, "The American people will never stand for this." Seeking a wider audience for his views he called the Union Club together in New York a few days later on March 26 and assailed Article Ten as "a trouble-breeder and not a peace-maker." He could see no good reason to accept "a guaranty to apply to unknown and unforeseeable contingencies" and preferred to "leave the future to conference and decision in the light of events." It was a grave mistake to hope that peace could be achieved by the "attempted enforcement of an inflexible rule." Rather peace must be ushered in by firm friendships based on a community of interests and purposes. Such friendship was more likely to grow from voluntary conferences called to meet specific emergencies than from "hard and fast engagements."[36]

As previously recounted, Hughes then sent Wilson seven proposed reservations including one eliminating Article Ten. Apparently Hughes did not work directly with Root, Hays, and Lodge in shaping Republican strategy. Root, especially, was gratified, however, that Hughes continued during the summer to hew so close to the party line. He hoped that someone would make Hughes' ideas known to the Senate.[37] Again without any apparent collusion Hughes gratified Root. In a letter to Senator Frederick Hale in July Hughes threw his weight behind the move for reservations. He called for changes eliminating those parts of the Covenant that threatened American independence, advocated keeping those features that provided for a judicial approach to peace, and advocated the immediate restoration of the economic community by adopting the Treaty of Versailles. His four reservations provided for withdrawal from the League, exclusion of domestic problems from League action, additional safeguards for the Monroe Doctrine, and a sharp modification in Article Ten. The United States would make a prior commitment to meet with the League Council but would reserve to itself all initiative. These changes, Hughes maintained, did not alter the essential character of the League. They did reach "a middle ground between aloofness and injurious commitment."[38]

The next month Hughes wrote Borah (no close friend), "the vice of Article X" was that it bound the United States to act without first conferring as to what the action ought to be. The Article should be made clearer or eliminated. If a reservation was employed, it ought to state plainly that the United States would undertake no obligation unless specifiically authorized by Congress and that Congress would be entirely free to exercise its own judgments as to discharging this obligation.[39]

Taft more than Hughes was dependent on Root in reaching his final conclusion to demand reservations to Article Ten. As President of the powerful League to Enforce Peace, Taft's opinions were in 1919 far more influential than those held by Hughes. Originally opposed to the use of force for peace, Taft, when he became active in the organization of the League to Enforce Peace from 1915 until the fall of 1919, favored military enforcement of arbitration. This was, of course, much less than Wilson sought in Article Ten. In March, 1919, Taft suggested amendments to the Covenant, but none to Article Ten, and subsequently found Wilson's amended League entirely satisfactory. For the *Covenanter*, a series of expositions of Wilson's work at Paris sponsored by the League to Enforce Peace, Taft chose to write a defense and explanation of Article Ten.[40] During May and June he worked against the addition of any crippling amendments or reservations to any article of the Covenant, his stand becoming the official policy of the League to Enforce Peace. Article Ten, now under Republican attack, he defended particularly. "It really is the heart of the League. It is the embodiment of what we fought for, and on it as a foundation rest the other provisions in the League to secure peace. It contains the primal essence of the League, which is the union of force in the world to suppress lawless force. . . ."[41]

To Arthur Vandenberg, at that time a newspaper editor, Taft wrote that Article Ten would impose no unreasonable burden, for the United States would in fact enforce the Article only in the Western Hemisphere—a duty no greater than that required by the Monroe Doctrine. In fact, since other League members would now join in supporting the Doctrine, America's responsibility would be lighter. The American Constitution was not in danger. Each individual nation, rather than the League Council, would decide how the obligation in Article Ten should be discharged. Consequently, in the United States the decision would rest with Congress, whose power to declare war remained unimpaired. Taft summed up his arguments with a reassuring conclusion. Article Ten constituted so serious a warning to aggressors that it would seldom, if ever, have to be put into use. There was here, Taft felt, an exact parallel to the Monroe Doctrine; its distinct warning that force would be used had made unnecessary any warfare to protect the Western Hemisphere.[42]

Taft continued his work by actively attempting to influence the Senate. He urged Senator Kellogg to take the lead in directing the League through the Senate without amendments. A great opportunity existed, Taft felt, for determined and intelligent leadership to refute the specious arguments of men like Borah and Knox.[43] Had Taft insisted on the views he held early in 1919 a split in Republican ranks would have been inevitable.

After the publication of Root's letter of June 21, however, Taft's support of Article Ten began to weaken. Possibly Wilson's failure to confer with and encourage him had much to do with his flagging zeal.[44] Will Hays, who was working closely with Lodge and Root, persuaded Taft, in July, to draft an amendment to Article Ten. He responded with a proposal to limit the life of the Article to five years. After this break, Taft's pronouncements on Article Ten became more confused and contradictory, while his support of reservations as the only means of securing ratification of the Treaty became more definite and strong.[45] Article Ten, Taft began to argue, was less important than the Treaty as a whole. For a time he attempted to reach a compromise by modifying Article Ten into a form satisfying to its enemies yet not offensive to its friends. In the atmosphere of 1919, charged with personal and partisan spite, such a moderate course was difficult to follow.

Taft's task was made more onerous because of his dislike of Wilson as a person and the Democrats as a party. Wilson he had earlier described as an opportunist who flopped from one policy to another defending each with ridiculous statements.[46] During the debate on the Treaty he wrote that the Democrats were making asses of themselves.[47]

Furthermore, the dislike for Wilson that Taft had always felt turned by 1920 to hatred and became a kind of obsession. The President's physical breakdown, Taft believed, was the result of his ruthless effort to take all the credit for the League. Taft had difficulty finding words to express his contempt for "that mulish enigma, that mountain of egotism and selfishness who lives in the White House."

At one time Taft had supported Article Ten with arguments very similar to Wilson's, even calling the Article "the heart of the Covenant." Further study led Taft to the conclusion that Article Ten was merely an important but not an indispensable part of the League. Wilson had forced the question to a choice between Article Ten and the League. Taft assumed that making peace in Europe, signing a treaty with our allies, and establishing some sort of a league were more important than the adoption of Article Ten which was no more than an "idea of Wilson's."[48] The use of force Taft had added to his peace plans as the last step. As he retreated, the use of the military was the first provision he was willing to relinquish. His conversion to force had grown from the urgency of war; the use of force had never been with him a basic article of faith. Uncertain in his convictions, he was drawn irresistibly by personal friendship and party loyalty to those men who had already repudiated Article Ten through crippling modifications. By mid-September Taft threw in his lot with the supporters of the Lodge reservations. Furthermore, while Taft did not glory in politics for its own sake, he did recognize that measures must be approved by men. Several times during the Senate debate he wrote Hitchcock urging compromise and warning the Democratic leader that the League without reservations had no possible chance for success. It was better, Taft wrote, to gain many of the general purposes of a league than to forfeit the whole plan to the futile hope that it might be ratified without reservations.[49]

Senator Lodge had the same opposition to Article Ten on principle that Root had, though it is difficult to clarify the Senator's real attitude. As a party leader it was expedient for him to subordinate personal convictions to the organization's welfare. His prime responsibility was to translate the violently conflicting opinions on the League within the Republican party into a single program on which Borah at one extreme and Le Baron Colt at the other could agree. Furthermore, Lodge's views on the merits of the League were colored by his intense dislike for Wilson.

Even so, Lodge was remarkably consistent, especially after January of 1917 when he opposed Wilson's embryonic association of nations, in his unwillingness to commit the nation to discharge obligations by force. While Lodge had declared in public speeches in 1915 and 1916 that peace must be enforced, as an old-line imperialist his conception of the use of force was limited to the nation acting in specific crises to safeguard definite national interests. A permanent pledge to maintain world order by restoring peace in disputes not directly threatening American interests was alien to his thinking. Nor did he think a pledge was practical, for he did not believe that nations would honor such commitments.

With these convictions were mixed the calculations of a shrewd politician. Lodge rejected the demands of Borah and Beveridge for a "flat denial" of the League. The proper course, Lodge suggested in the fall of 1918, with the approval of Roosevelt and Root, was to accept the purpose of the

League—peace—but reject its methods. Indeed, he added, the "strength of our position is to show the impossibility of any of the methods proposed."[50] For example, any practical league that involved the control of American armies and navies or the establishment of an international police would raise an issue, said Lodge, on which "we shall win." A few days later he explained this point in detail. The League was a vague and attractive title. Republicans must make clear to the people that a league must make decisions which must be enforced at great sacrifice.

Americans were fascinated by the idea of eternal world peace; it was their first thought, but they would never accept the obligation of Article Ten, Lodge wrote. Enthusiasm would quickly cool when the people were shown that in the League plan "one single clause requires us to guarantee the territorial integrity and political independence of every nation on earth." Such a guarantee could be sustained only by military might. And, added Lodge, "The second thought of the people will be for us. . . ."[51]

Lodge, however, wrote that Article Ten was not simply a question of personal fortune or party advantage to most senators "but a great question of principle on which they cannot yield any essential point."[52] The overwhelming opinion in the Senate was against a league with compulsive force behind it. Nor did Lodge believe reservations would save the League. Wilson for his part did not mean "to yield anything at all."

Lodge's position as he stated it in March was not to oppose "a league which would be safe and help keep the peace of the world and not injure the United States. . . ." This, by his earlier statements, was a league without Article Ten.[53] Lodge seems to have believed honestly that the League would lead to war rather than peace. In March he became convinced that the American people agreed with him. His mail, which was large enough to be indicative of the trend of public opinion, indicated a continually mounting opposition to the League. At first the majority of his correspondents favored the League, but the tide had turned until in March the count was ten to one opposing it.[54] This drift of public opinion was significant for, as Lodge himself said, his first duty was not so much to judge the League on its merits as to make those

political decisions that would hold together the Republican
majority in the Senate.[55]

Apparently, Lodge began to feel in March and April,
while Wilson was making amendments to the Covenant, that
a league might be politically expedient. He weakened enough
to cause some of the irreconcilables concern. Even then,
Beveridge did not think Lodge would yield, for the Senator
realized he represented a cause as well as a party. In April,
Beveridge was able to write, "My confidence in Lodge
grows all of the time."[56] And well it might, for Lodge was
then enlisting the aid of Root in demanding a league with
reservations. Even before these plans were made public in
June, Beveridge believed the fight was won.[57]

After the Root letter of June 21 the clamor for reservations
in and out of the Senate grew stronger and at the same
time so did Lodge's determination. It was still impossible, he
wrote in August, to defeat the League in an outright vote
because the Treaty and the League were bound together.
Great progress had been made since April, however, and
Republicans were united on strong reservations "along the
lines indicated by Mr. Root." The irreconcilables were con-
stantly gaining strength; sentiment to defeat the treaty outright was growing. This trend Lodge ascribed to the public
distrust aroused as a closer study of the Treaty revealed secret
agreements, furtive bargains, and alliances for war.

At this time Lodge reiterated his opposition to Article Ten
in unmistakable terms. He would have supported the League
if Article Ten had been left out and a guarantee for France
inserted.[58] To irreconcilables who feared the reservation to
Article Ten was not sweeping enough, he explained that "the
Senate in the reservation refuses its consent to Article 10. It
could do no more by striking it out." Reservations, he added,
"change the treaty and relieve us of obligation."[59] The next
month he declared that he would kill Article Ten and
preserve the Treaty if possible. If not, he would kill the
Treaty as well.[60] His one desire, however, was "to get the
United States out of dangerous complications." By early
September he believed that the Treaty would pass. The Republicans would stand firm in demanding the reservations.
The Democrats seeing this would accept the reservations
rather than let the Treaty die.[61]

The Republican party in the Senate, led by the wisdom of Root and the parliamentary skill of Lodge, had built a platform on which all members could stand—the League with substantive reservations. It is fruitless to seek to measure the motives of these leaders. Perhaps they had no designs beyond partisan profit. It can be said, however, that they had honest misgivings about Article Ten. Distrust of Article Ten, significantly, had been reflected at Paris by all members of the American delegation. Their reactions and objections even though they favored Wilson or were wholly disinterested were similar to the popular and partisan criticism expressed in the heated debate at home.

A venerated tradition had become obsolete the President maintained. Leaders of American opinion in both parties were not sure that Wilson's thesis was justified. In the Senate, where traditions were supreme, the natural antipathy for innovation was intensified by the inherent suspicion of executive authority. When the Executive displayed unwillingness to accept the Senate's traditional mode of operation—compromise—Wilson's chance of putting the League through the Senate became slight. It was not a matter of adjusting a few differences or forgetting personal animosities. Wilson was challenging tradition; he was challenging the Senate.

CHAPTER VI

Wilson Considers Compromise

FROM the outset of the treaty negotiations Wilson placed little faith in his ability to win the support of the Senate directly. His hard-won reservations to the Covenant at Paris he undertook in the hope that they would clear doubts from the public mind and insure a wave of public support which would sweep Senate opposition aside. Supremely confident of his ability to arouse the people to support reform, he considered seriously taking his case directly to the people in a cross-country campaign as soon as the Conference ended. A tentative itinerary was drawn up and the substance of the speeches discussed.[1] Such a tour would be a direct challenge to the Senate, a test of strength. Wilson argued, however, that the only way to handle the Senate was by "making a direct frontal attack in reply. Article X is the king pin of the whole structure . . . without it, the Covenant would mean nothing. If the Senate will not accept that, it will have to reject the whole treaty. It is manifestly too late now to effect changes in the Covenant. . . ." Wilson hoped that his friends would join him in the "most militant and aggressive course" which he meant to undertake the "minute I get back."[2]

The Senate reaction to his formal presentation of the Treaty on July 10 did little to change the President's mind. Harding characterized the address as "utterly lacking in ringing Americanism," while Senator Brandegee dismissed it as "soap bubbles of oratory and soufflé of phrases."[3] Nevertheless, Wilson's advisors, in particular House and Lansing, continued to argue that a tour of the nation would be political folly, alienating the Republican "mild reservationists" who might be won to the Wilson camp by conciliation. The President reluctantly agreed to postpone indefinitely his tour of the West and make an effort, to which he devoted much time in July and August, toward winning over senators by persuasion.

In retrospect, at least, the work of these days seems the height of futility. Two fundamental issues, neither subject to compromise, separated the President and the Senate. In the first place, he would not accept rejection or even modification of the obligation inherent in Article Ten. "We ought to go in or to stay out," he said. The Article was the heart of the Covenant because it was the measure of the nation's sincerity and responsibility in joining the League. Formal membership with faint-hearted support indicated failure to grasp the revolution necessary in American foreign policy. In the second place, Wilson had a firm conviction, possibly because it added great weight to his argument, that substantive reservations to the Covenant would require the consent of the other signatories. All of this would mean renegotiation of the Treaty for he did not believe the United States had the authority to make changes alone. With the tortuous days at Paris still fresh in his mind, he was certain attempts at renegotiation would result in demands by foreign nations for new concessions. Chaos and failure would be the certain fate of such a conference. Furthermore, substantive changes in the form of a treaty, Wilson wrote, "seem to me to belong to the powers of negotiation which belong to the President. . . ." Even if the Senate had passed the Treaty with the substantive Lodge reservations attached—the only form in which it had a chance to gain approval—Wilson felt so strongly on these two matters that he would have, according to his private statements, withdrawn the Treaty and in effect vetoed ratification.[4] There was, of course, nothing unique about Wilson's position. Theodore Roosevelt had threatened the same action in 1905 when the Senate added reservations to the pending arbitration treaties and Taft pigeonholed the 1911 arbitration treaties after the Senate altered them drastically. The League issue was vastly more important than the arbitration treaties had been, but Wilson's reaction and strategy were the same as followed by earlier presidents.[5]

The extreme concession that Wilson was willing to make was to accept interpretative reservations not attached to the Treaty itself. In this form statements of the understanding of the obligations involved in the Covenant could be made without the consent of other signatories. This was not a small concession on the part of the President. If a substantial number of senators really favored Article Ten, but honestly desired to make clear that it would not alter the American constitutional system, an interpretative reservation would have been sufficient.

Interpretative reservations were not enough, for the opposition to Article Ten ran too deep. It was true that there was in the Senate an "insane hatred" for Wilson that turned many of its members into "a snarling pack of madmen" determined to "mortify and humiliate" Wilson;[6] with these men any path of concession would probably have been endless. Acceptance of a reservation would have led to the substitution of a more drastic and unacceptable reservation. But even in the highly charged atmosphere of the debate marked by exaggeration and conscious attempts to mislead, the fact remains that there was little enthusiasm, either by Republicans or Democrats, for Article Ten. More significant than the flat denunciation of the Article by irreconcilables was the demand by nearly all of the mild reservationists to alter its terms or interpret it into something innocuous. With the Democrats who voted for an unreserved Article Ten, party loyalty, more often than personal conviction, dictated decision. The senators who defended Article Ten condemned it with faint praise. Their cautious and negative arguments proclaimed no bold new era in American foreign policy. Rather they accepted the Article as an extension of American traditions in a commitment which would seldom, if ever, have to be executed. In terms of Wilson's vision of collective security, the Senate support of Article Ten was scarcely less damaging than the opposition attack.

Few senators supporting Article Ten were willing to accept its full implications. Senator Claude A. Swanson, for example, seemed to favor Article Ten only because he expected it to remain inactive. A pledge to use force would insure peace; the actual use of force under Article Ten would be unnecessary. It would, asserted Swanson, function as the Monroe Doctrine had functioned. In that case, the announced intention of the United States to oppose external aggression had been sufficient to protect the entire Western

Hemisphere for a century without actual force ever having to be used.[7]

Even more violence to the true principle of Article Ten was inflicted in the defense given by Senator Porter J. McCumber, one of its few Republican supporters. By his interpretation the affirmative guarantee to preserve the territorial integrity of nations was made a negative guarantee not to violate the territory of other countries. Article Ten, said McCumber, was an agreement not to go to war for an unlawful purpose. "If we do not agree that we will not make a war of aggression against another nation, then what is this peace talk about?"[8]

A few senators understood the true purpose of Article Ten and supported its provisions. Senator John F. Nugent, for one, declared that even if 500,000 American soldiers had to be stationed in Europe, as Lodge predicted, it was still a small price to pay for peace. It would be an infinitely smaller penalty than the sacrifice of the million men it would take to restore peace once war broke out. Article Ten as interpreted by Senator Robert L. Owen was not a break with American tradition, but the extension into foreign affairs of one of the most important of American traditions—the Monroe Doctrine. That Doctrine was not, as some maintained, a license to overlordship of the hemisphere. It was the statement of a purpose to defend the hemisphere from injustice and imperialism.[9] Senator Marcus A. Smith argued that the Monroe Doctrine was as much a pledge to go to war as Article Ten. The United States, furthermore, was not violating tradition by guaranteeing the independence of a foreign state. It had done so for years in its treaty with Panama. The United States would not have sole responsibility for executing the Article. The burden would fall equally on all members.[10]

Probably the most cogent defense of Article Ten, at least in terms of Wilson's ideals, was made by Senator Thomas J. Walsh of Montana. He refuted, at least to his own satisfaction, most of the specific charges against it. Peaceful change was possible under Article Ten. Its guarantee was against "external aggression." Throughout history conquest had accounted for little in the way of legitimate and constructive change in international affairs. There were almost no instances of a nation gratuitously extending aid to a revolutionary movement. The right of revolution, he believed, was in no way impaired.

The most important part of the Covenant was Article Ten, declared Walsh: "It is because it is such that those who, for one reason or another, wish to see the proposed plan defeated or rendered ineffective, if adopted, desire to emasculate Article 10 by 'Amendments.' " Article Ten would prevent war. It would preserve peace as the Monroe Doctrine had preserved peace—by declaring that the United States would "make war upon any European nation that should attempt to violate the soil of an American republic; because we voluntarily and without any reciprocal agreement or other consideration bound ourselves and avowed our purpose to 'preserve as against external aggression the territorial integrity and political independence of' the Western Hemisphere."

Congress did not lose any of its authority as a result of the Article, continued Walsh. The moral obligation did not bind the United States to automatic action. Each case would require a decision made by Congress. If the United States Congress did not feel that a certain case brought before the League Council justified action by the United States, no action need be taken. Even if Congress decided to act, war was not inevitable. Economic boycott, for instance, would probably meet the need. The League was not an instrument of war but an attempt "to add, in the case of nations, the coercion which even primitive man found essential to his welfare in the case of members of his little community."

In conclusion, Walsh admitted the weakness of the League in the cruel pre-war world. The use of force, dangerous in a world ruled by autocratic monarchs, immersed in intrigue and obsessed by the idea of conquest, was wholly safe in a post-war world of self-governing democracies. Peace could be maintained by force through an agreement such as Article Ten or by the establishment of an international police force. Walsh chose Article Ten.[11]

While these feeble voices were being raised against the fusillade of attack on Article Ten, while the Republican party united on a program of the League with reservations, Wilson worked to stem the deluge that threatened to sweep him to defeat. On July 15 he wrote to eight Republican "mild reservationists" asking for an opportunity to talk with them about the Treaty and later spent hours in individual conversation with them. His slight chances for success were diminished further by the wide publicity given to these conferences. Any senator who agreed to concessions appeared to be admitting a fault.[12] At the same time that Wilson was seeing the "mild reservationists" Root was giving them conflicting interpretations of the Treaty while Hays was urging them to stand firm with the party for political reasons. Accustomed to thinking of senators as devils, Wilson soon came to doubt the sincerity of the mild reservationists and became convinced that they were attempting to humiliate him. By the end of July Wilson sensed that he was losing the initiative and being pushed into a defensive position.

In spite of these evident failures, advisors still urged Wilson to compromise. Lansing by August, 1919, was convinced, even more than before, that to insist on a treaty without reservations was to invite almost certain defeat. The Treaty could not be driven through the Senate by "sheer force"; it was time "to catch flies with honey." A few days later the Secretary of State appeared before the Senate Foreign Relations Committee to testify on the Treaty. Lansing's personal feelings toward Wilson were cool at the time. Nevertheless, he was appalled at the evident desire of the senators, in this public hearing, to embarrass Wilson rather than to gain information. Convinced of the vital need for conciliation by this experience, Lansing told the President, August 11, that the Senate would never accept the Treaty without reservations. The President's proposed Western tour, Lansing warned, rather than improving the League's chance of acceptance, would invite disaster. Mild reservationists in the Senate, whose support Wilson needed, would be offended at his effort to appeal over their heads to the people.[13] By August, however, Lansing's influence on Wilson was slight.

Wilson had not abandoned all hope of winning the mild reservationists to his position: interpretative reservations incorporated into a separate resolution distinct from the Treaty itself. Speaking to the Senate Committee on Foreign Relations, August 19, Wilson described Article Ten as the very backbone of the whole Covenant; a league without this provision would "be hardly more than an influential debating society."

Yet, said the President in answer to a question by Senator McCumber, there could be no objection to the substance of an interpretative reservation stating that Congress might use its own judgment under Article Ten rather than automatically following the decisions of the League Council. "We differ, Senator, only as to the form of action." The United States had every right to interpret its moral obligations under Article Ten. But, insisted Wilson, "it would be a very serious practical mistake to put it in the resolution of ratification," for then the Treaty would have to be resubmitted to the powers for ratification. Unfortunately no final and authoritative statement was universally accepted as to the form of reservations. Wilson failed to convince the mild reservationists.

More important, perhaps, was the President's inability to give a compelling interpretation of American responsibilities under Article Ten. Senator Brandegee probed the nature of the obligation in Article Ten with complex questions designed to confuse Wilson. Brandegee suggested that the obligation in Article Ten was in the nature of a legal contract leaving no discretion or judgment to Congress as to its execution. Wilson denied this view and insisted that the obligation was moral and therefore included an element of judgment. In a legal obligation no element of judgment was involved after the contract was drawn. Under Article Ten Congress would have the power to judge each incident on its own merits; it could act or refuse to act as it saw fit. Further the United States held a veto on disputes to which it was not a party. Then the wily Brandegee insisted that Article Ten would be meaningless if each nation could decide for itself whether to honor its contract. That any "terror to wrongdoers" would evolve from such an agreement he could not see. In vain Wilson insisted that a moral obligation was binding. Congress had the right to exercise independent judgment in every crisis in foreign affairs. In most, if not all, cases Congress would decide to discharge the obligations under Article Ten. Nothing was settled by this exchange of opinions, of course. If the obligation was legal, Congress had no freedom of choice; if the obligation was moral, Congress was under no compulsion to act. No senators were won to Wilson's side.

It was of utmost significance that Wilson failed to establish the distinction in obligations even to the satisfaction of his strong supporter and close friend, Senator John Sharp Williams, who felt that Wilson's explanations were superfluous because "all international obligations are moral ones." To say that Article Ten was "a legal obligation with a moral sanction" availed nothing. When distinctions became so refined, they became meaningless to the Senate or to the people. A compelling, easily understood defense was essential to gain support for Wilson's uncompromising position on Article Ten. Wilson failed, for his argument impressed the public as unnecessary straining at trifles.[14]

The only other important point relating to Article Ten brought out by the Committee's questioning was its authorship. Wilson freely accepted all responsibility. Tracing the Article's origin back to the Pan-American Treaty, he acknowledged no debt to anyone else in framing its provisions. Authorship and the nature of the obligations under Article Ten provided much of the subject for debate in the Senate on the League.

Shortly after this conference Wilson, who had considered a nationwide tour as early as March, made his final decision to take his case to the people. His attempts to win over the mild reservationists in the Senate had shown little results; even if he offended them by appealing over their heads to the people, nothing would be lost. Thoroughly aroused by the intractability of senators, Wilson declared that if they wanted war, he would "give them a belly full."[15]

Before leaving for his Western tour, Wilson drafted four interpretative reservations, including one on Article Ten. These were left with Senator Hitchcock who was to use them as a basis of compromise if it became necessary to do so, but he was sworn not to make public Wilson's authorship. This robbed the reservations of an official character and rendered them of limited effectiveness in the actual debate. In these reservations Wilson wrote of Article Ten: "It [the United States] understands that the advice of the Council of the League with regard to the employment of armed force contemplated in Article Ten of the Covenant of the League is to be regarded only as advice and leaves each member State free to exercise its own judgment as to whether it is wise or practicable to act upon that advice or

not." Hitchcock in the debate that followed used this proposal with the added stipulation that Congress alone could
accept the advice of the League Council and had the authority to declare war.[16]

Many reasons have been advanced for Wilson's unyielding
and uncompromising tone in his cross-country speeches. One
explanation is that this strong stand was the first half of a
political plan, halted in mid-career by Wilson's collapse. On
the tour the President would demand the extreme. Then when
compromise became inevitable he would yield as little as
possible while moving toward the interpretative reservations
left with Hitchcock.[17] Wilson in July had told Wiseman con-
fidentially that it might be necessary to accept interpretations of language in certain articles. If so, he was determined
to drive a hard bargain. Concession would be called weakness;
he would concede nothing until forced to do so.[18]

Wilson may have taken an extreme position because he
underestimated the true temper of the forces opposing him
and believed he could carry his point. Herbert Hoover was
amazed that Wilson seemed oblivious to the marked personal antipathy that so many of the European statesmen felt
toward him at Paris. Lansing wrote that the tour would be
a futile mission; Wilson did not grasp the intensity of the
personal hatred his enemies nurtured nor recognize that it
was widespread, not limited to political enemies in the
Senate.[19] Yet Wilson himself understood only too well the
measure of personal hatred that surrounded him. "If I had
nothing to do with the League of Nations it would go
through," he remarked after his tour was over.[20]

Houston, another member of Wilson's cabinet, thought
that the President greatly overestimated the degree of popular
demand for the League. Regarding it as a moral issue he believed the people would come to understand it in that light,
and when they did, they would support the League against
all odds.[21] As he had during the war drawn a distinction between the German people and their leaders, he believed now
that the Senate in its opinions on the League was infinitely
remote from the mass of the American people.

Actually, Wilson did not make his tour as a carefully
calculated move sure to bring victory. He felt driven to do
everything possible to avert defeat and a public campaign
was the only remaining possibility.

One simple but significant fact was clear from May, 1916, when Wilson made the League a definite part of his policy: he never believed that the Senate would willingly accept his plan for an affirmative guarantee; the guarantee was the essential of a new world order; consequently, the affirmative guarantee would have to be forced roughshod over the protesting Senate. Following this theory Wilson refused to invite Senate resolutions in 1916 on a league. The Senate seemed to confirm Wilson's fears when it refused to approve references to an association of nations in his address of January 22, 1917, on the terms of peace. The President thereafter refused to announce a definite plan for a league and submit it to public debate in 1918 and 1919. Instead, he sought, by making the League an integral part of the Treaty, to crush opposition under the weight of popular demand for immediate peace. A wiser politician might possibly have altered these long-standing plans in the face of rising opposition.

But it was not Wilson's nature to compromise where principles were at stake. Illness may have intensified but certainly did not account for his inflexible course in 1919-1920. Rationally and deliberately he insisted on universal collective security and on Article Ten because he was convinced it represented not a minor technical difference of opinion with Senate reservationists, but the difference between success or failure of the League. It was consistent with his whole character that he "spurned the role of statesman for what he must have thought was the nobler role of prophet."[22]

CHAPTER VII

Compromise Rejected

THE revolution in American foreign policy that had been unfolding since 1916 reached its climax in the September days of 1919. There would be, when it was too late, renewed efforts at compromise, but for the next few weeks the President and the Senate leaders stood firmly by their polar positions on Article Ten. The Senate campaign got under way with the report on September 10 of the Senate Committee on Foreign Relations recommending ratification of the Covenant with reservations, and ended when the proposal was defeated in November. For Wilson the active campaign was limited to the twenty-two days from September 3, when he brushed aside the warnings of friends with the words "I must go," to September 25, when he closed his last speech at Pueblo by saying: "We have accepted the truth and we are going to be led by it, and it is going to lead us, and through us the world, out into pastures of quietness and peace such as the world never dreamed of before."

It is difficult to reduce to a few words Wilson's arguments during his tour in favor of Article Ten for he spoke on the topic many times and framed his arguments to suit many different audiences. A few major ideas, however, emerge. The indispensable Article Ten did not, Wilson maintained, constitute a break with American traditional foreign policy. It was, in his firm conviction, the logical evolution and crowning confirmation of American ideals in foreign policy—an extension of the Monroe Doctrine to the world—rather than a dangerous experiment. Certainly it was not an entangling alliance. Again and again he asserted the principle: "There is no entangling alliance in a concert of power. When all unite to act in the same sense and with the same purpose all act in the common interest and are free to live under a common protection."[1]

96

The increased responsibility and obligation inherent in Article Ten were necessary to meet the world duty imposed upon the United States by its growth to world power. The need to assume such broad commitments Wilson sought to justify, as he had America's war aims, in terms of the nation's duty to humanity rather than relying on the more expedient argument of maintaining national security. Indeed, a permanent peace had been America's ultimate war aim. Frequently he asked, "Shall the great sacrifice that we made in the war be in vain . . . ?" Unfortunately the appeal to idealism, worn thin by heavy sacrifices of war, became less compelling as the nation's crusading fire faded.

Wilson never failed to stress the absolute necessity for the nation to assume the ultimate responsibility of Article Ten—the use of force to preserve peace. There would be reliance on moral coercion, but if the moral forces of the world could not prevail, Wilson asserted, "the physical forces of the world shall." There must be a definite assurance of peace through an absolute guarantee against aggression.

Wilson realized he was raising a high call to duty; nevertheless the burden of responsibility would not, as his critics charged, be overwhelming. The very act of pledging the use of force would in itself be so stern a warning to aggressors as largely to obviate the need to use force. When aggression threatened, the League would call for arbitration. After a case was submitted, at least nine months must pass before a decision could be rendered. During this time the restraining force of public opinion might well shame a would-be aggressor into a peaceful settlement. If these measures failed, the League would apply Article Sixteen, the most complete economic boycott ever conceived of in a public document. "I want to say to you with confident prediction that there will be no fighting after that."[2] Indeed, Wilson asserted, the economic embargo would, in time, become a substitute for war and make the use of force obsolete.

Even if these deterrents to aggression failed, enforcement of the pledge in Article Ten would not require the United States to police the world. Enforcement would begin at the regional level. "If you want to put out a fire in Utah, you do not send to Oklahoma for the engine. If you want to put out a fire in the Balkans . . . you do not send to the United

States for troops." The League Council would select the most available "fireman" and, it was important to note, send him only after gaining his consent.[3]

There were no apparent threats to peace in the Western Hemisphere where the United States would have responsibility. European states alone, in the normal course of events, would settle European squabbles. Hence, the United States would not, as a result of Article Ten, become involved in war unless there developed a conflict of such major proportions that neutrality would be impossible in any event. The League, Wilson was fond of saying, was a "constitution of Peace, not a league of War."[4]

Wilson attacked as well as refuted his critics. The opponents of Article Ten he characterized as persons who objected "to entering the League with any responsibilities whatever." Congress did not, as they asserted, lose under Article Ten any of its power to declare war. The charge by opponents of the Article that United States armies could be ordered abroad by some other power or by a combination of powers was false and, added Wilson, they knew it was false. European nations would not wish to have their armies ordered into action by the United States; they were just as jealous of their own sovereignty as the American people were of theirs.

The talk of the League as a supergovernment and the need for reservations to protect the United States from its tyranny under Article Ten Wilson ridiculed. "No active policy can be undertaken by the League without the assenting vote of the Council." The "affirmative vote of the United States is in every instance necessary. . . no active policy can be undertaken by the League without the assenting vote of the United States." The League could not on its own authority interfere with domestic or foreign policies of the United States. "We would be under our own direction just as much under the Covenant of the League of Nations as we are now. . . ."[5]

America was afforded every legal protection of its interests. But beyond legalities lay the spirit of the League of Nations, to Wilson vastly more significant. The Lodge reservation to Article Ten was legally inconsequential. It provided protection already extended in the body of the

Covenant. Thus it could be argued from the legal point of view that the Lodge reservation was unnecessary but harmless. Yet to Wilson it seemed that the reservation constituted a grave danger to the spirit of the League. If Americans accepted the Lodge reservation to Article Ten, they declared their intention to honor their pledge to preserve world peace only when it suited their purpose to do so. "We will not promise anything, but from time to time we may cooperate. We will not assume any obligations." The "unworthy and ridiculous" Lodge reservation, while legally innocuous, would in fact render the entire League meaningless and amount to nothing less than the total rejection of the Covenant. "It means," asserted Wilson," that the United States would take from under the structure its very foundations and support."

One of Wilson's most complete explanations of the meaning and significance of Article Ten, and a good example of his oratory, was the September 3 speech in St. Louis, Missouri, at the start of his ill-fated national tour. It was an impassioned plea to avert the doom which nullification of Article Ten would seal. "When you read Article X, therefore, you will see," he told his audience, "that it is nothing but the inevitable, logical center of the whole system of the Covenant of the League of Nations, and I stand for it absolutely. If it should in any important respect be impaired, I would feel like asking the Secretary of War to get the boys who went across the water to fight together on some field where I could go and see them, and I would stand up before them and say, 'Boys, I told you before you went across the seas that this was a war against wars, and I did my best to fulfill the promise, but I am obliged to come to you in mortification and shame and say I have not been able to fulfill the promise. You are betrayed. You fought for something you did not get! And the glory of the Armies and the Navies of the United States is gone like a dream in the night, and there issues upon it, in the suitable darkness of the night, the nightmare of dread which lay upon the nations before this war came; and there will come sometime, in the vengeful Providence of God, another struggle in which, not a few hundred thousand fine men from America will have to die, but as many millions as are necessary to accomplish the final freedom of the peoples of the world.' "[6]

There was no doubt in the mind of the gaunt leader, who continued his crusade day after day despite the handicaps of sickness and fatigue, that American isolation was in fact at an end. The genius of the people, the vast growth of the nation, had made America a determining power in world affairs. "After you have become a determining factor you cannot remain isolated, whether you want to or not."[7] For his part Wilson was ready and anxious to "accept what is offered to us, the leadership of the world": a leadership "not of exploiting power, but of liberating power, a power to show the world that when America was born it was indeed a finger pointed toward those lands into which men could deploy . . . and live in happy freedom"; a leadership that would bring to reality the dream of a civilization, no longer decimated by wars, where men "should govern themselves in peace and amity and quiet." That leadership America had coveted; now the world offered it. To the orator on the platform, his eyes on the future, it was "inconceivable that we should reject it."[8]

What did those throngs of people who listened intently to Wilson understand and think of the new destiny of leadership, the new era of world responsibility to which he called them? What did the ninety-six members of the United States Senate think of this new definition of America's foreign policy? It was the essence of the political system Wilson revered that he could not go beyond the will of the people or the Senate.

The Senate was growing more obdurate and bold each day in its opposition to the League without reservations. The leaders sensed that public opinion was moving with them and that in defending proved tradition against Wilson's untested theories they had a marked advantage.

Indeed, the Republican opposition in the Senate was growing so strong that Root, its guiding force, became alarmed and warned Lodge not to let the irreconcilables take control, as now seemed likely, by advocating strong reservations designed to defeat the Treaty. If the Republican reservationists became suspicious of the irreconcilables, party unity might be shattered with disastrous results. Root urged Lodge to exert every effort to reunite the Republican ranks by checking the irreconcilables.[9] Lodge may have taken this advice for there was no rift in his party ranks. If so, he did it without weakening the reservations. They must be strong, he explained in defending his action. Opposition had grown much more determined than Root realized and without strong reservations the Treaty would fail.[10]

The first concrete result of all of the Root-Lodge labors was announced on September 10 in the recommendation of the Senate Committee on Foreign Relations for four reservations to the League. In three of these the influence of Root was evident. They provided the right of unconditional withdrawal from the League, exclusive American control over domestic affairs, and exclusion of the Monroe Doctrine from the jurisdiction of the League. A fourth reservation dealing with Article Ten did not provide the outright rejection Root advocated. Its terms he approved, however, believing it achieved essentially the same end by virtually nullifying the Article. In this opinion Lodge concurred. Just after these reservations were announced Lodge said privately that he sought to kill Article Ten, and if he failed he would kill the entire Treaty.[11]

The Committee in its explanation of the reservation to Article Ten stated, "This reservation is intended to meet the most vital objection to the League covenant as it stands. Under no circumstances must there be any legal or moral obligation upon the United States to enter into war or send its Army and Navy abroad or without the unfettered action of Congress to impose economic boycotts on other countries. Under the Constitution of the United States the Congress alone has the power to declare war." Lodge thought that this statement, later incorporated in the reservation proper, "in a general way . . . sums up the objections to Article Ten as presented by Mr. Wilson." From the beginning of the debate, Lodge declared, the majority of the Senate would not accept Wilson's version of Article Ten.[12]

Public reaction to the speeches on Wilson's Western tour was closely watched by Senator Lodge. The results encouraged him. Anderson was told that the more drastic reservations were being held back and might not be needed. Their use, said Lodge, would be unnecessary if it became feasible to get rid of the League entirely, as now seemed possible.[13]

Lodge, meanwhile, continued his efforts to get all Republicans to agree on the reservation to Article Ten. Senator McCumber was the most difficult to convince, the last to yield. Kellogg and Lodge advised with him for ten days. Both saw him on September 22, when he accepted, at last, the reservation in the form it took when presented to the Senate and finally adopted.[14] Although the conferences were supposedly confidential, a draft of this reservation inexplicably was in Wilson's hands the next day. Kellogg thought McCumber must have given it to Hitchcock who in turn telegraphed it to Wilson.[15] Lodge's comment was that the draft "in some way" reached Wilson. However Wilson got the draft, it was most fortunate for the Republicans that he did get it.

The President, in Salt Lake City on September 23, read, in the course of his speech, the entire Senate reservation to Article Ten. "That," he declared, "is a rejection of the covenant. That is an absolute refusal to carry any part of the same responsibility that the other members of the League carry. This [Article 10] is the heart of the covenant."[16] The President's flat rejection of the Lodge reservation to Article Ten on September 23 was most significant for it was one of his final statements. On the last day of the tour, September 25, Wilson asserted publicly, as he had done privately to Tumulty in June, that he would not ratify the Treaty with substantive reservations even if the Senate approved it.[17] From this position the President did not retreat. Hitchcock, after a conference with him on November 17, announced that Wilson would pocket the Treaty unless the Lodge reservation to Article Ten was altered.[18]

After Wilson's public rejection of the reservation his "extreme, almost violent feeling . . . in regard to Article 10" Lodge attributed to a degree of pride in authorship that made the President unwilling to accept any change in wording. Lodge concluded later that Article Ten had been "the storm center of the debate and did more than all other provisions put together to defeat the treaty. . . ."[19]

Wilson, unfortunately, was not as aware as he might have been had his health not failed that such forces as American nationalism and Irish-American nationalism made some type of reservation to Article Ten imperative. Shut off as he was from the outside world Wilson continued to feel, as he always had, that the Lodge reservation served no useful purpose and nullified Article Ten by removing from it any moral obligation to exercise restraint on an aggressor and thus destroying the cardinal principle in Wilson's theory of collective security.

As the time for the vote on the Treaty approached, two alternatives to the Lodge reservation to Article Ten were unsuccessfully promoted. The first was proposed on November 10 by Senator Borah in a reservation specifically freeing the United States from any legal or moral obligation under Article Ten. So frank and complete a nullification of the Article was voted down 68 to 18.[20] The second alternative to the Lodge reservation was suggested by Senator Hitchcock and provided interpretative reservations to five articles, including Article Ten. This proposal, which had Wilson's secret support, was not even acceptable enough to the Senate to be brought to a vote.[21] Possibly if Wilson had been well and able to work for these reservations after his tour, they would have received more consideration.

The Senate on November 13 voted to accept the Lodge reservation to Article Ten. Of the vote Lodge declared that "the line was sharply drawn, and it was really the test vote on the adoption of what was known as the 'Lodge Reservations.' "[22] All the Republicans present and four Democrats united to carry the reservation by 46 to 33 votes.[23]

On the face of the reservation to Article Ten the Constitutional authority of Congress to declare war was protected. In view of the fact that congressional approval for military action has been in later years required in such efforts at collective security as the United Nations and the North Atlantic Treaty, the reservation does not seem to alter Article Ten unreasonably. The words of the statement, however, are largely meaningless if considered outside the context of the 1920's. There was no reason to believe that Congress in 1919 or for a long time thereafter would authorize the use of military force in behalf of the League Covenant. Indeed, nothing in the diplomatic history of the United States during the next two decades invalidated this assumption. Root, who felt that accepting Article Ten "would be to surrender the moral power of the United States in favor of justice which is the only sure basis of peace," was satisfied with the reservation because he believed that it nullified Article Ten. Wilson, who believed that Article Ten was the "heart of the covenant" and represented America's willingness to make the "supreme sacrifice of throwing in our fortunes with the fortunes of men everywhere," also believed the reservation nullified Article Ten and was, therefore, "a rejection of the covenant." He did not accept the reservation; he could not accept it.

A few days later the Treaty and the League were rejected in the Senate. When the vote had been taken, a group of Republicans met in Lodge's office to hold what Hays described as a "wake." After remarking, "We did the best we could," Lodge took a picture of himself from his desk drawer, autographed it, along with the date, November 19, 1919, and handed it to Hays.[24]

Senators began at once seeking to reach a compromise on the reservations to the League. There was very little chance for such a move to succeed. Lansing believed that the Democrats would have to initiate any compromise and agree to alter Article Ten. There was little disposition, he feared, to meet either requirement.[25]

Possibly the real situation was even more hopeless than Lansing suspected. Before the defeat of the Treaty Hitchcock had urged Wilson to compromise. But the President had answered, "Let Lodge compromise." When Hitchcock persisted and suggested that "we might hold out the olive branch," Wilson replied, "Let Lodge hold out the olive branch."[26] The defeat of the Treaty failed to soften Wilson's opinions. The failure of the Treaty was the "undivided responsibility" of Republican leaders in the Senate. Consequently it would be a serious mistake, an admission of guilt "for our side to propose anything."[27]

Nor was there much chance that the Senate Republicans would make serious proposal for compromise. Anderson explained privately to friends in December that the Senate's only interest was to secure the protection afforded by reservations should the Treaty be ratified, and the Senate "would not be disappointed if the whole thing was defeated."[28] Anderson's personal advice, as expressed to Lord Grey, was to abandon all idea of a league of nations. The

Constitution made it impossible for the United States to participate in an international executive council. Instead, there should be established a court of arbitration to deal with legal problems and an international advisory council, in distinction to an executive council, to treat with political problems.[29] In these views Anderson no doubt reflected the opinion of many of the leaders in the Republican party.

Certainly the irreconcilable opponents of the League were not inclined to compromise or accept responsibility for the Covenant's failure. Brandegee, for example, placed the entire blame on Wilson and feared that he would attempt to "shuffle" the Lodge reservations in order to make them his own, get the Treaty passed, and claim a victory. In this sort of compromise the President might be aided, Brandegee warned, by the Republican mild reservationist, "a gelatinous type" with "a melting point slightly above zero, who so long as they were supported by Root and Taft and other high brows" would "continue to bleat for compromise." "The time for compromise has passed. We have the advantage now. The Democrats have killed the Treaty. . . ."[30]

Root, however, raised a voice in favor of moderation. The party platform, as he had proposed it, was for the League with reservations; the party, nevertheless, had not accepted all of his advice. The Republican irreconcilables voted for each of the reservations but against the League with reservations. Thus the logic of the argument that Republicans wanted a league, provided it was safeguarded by reservations, was destroyed. The Republican irreconcilables were using reservations, it was evident, to defeat rather than to ratify the League. (It was precisely against this danger that Root had warned Lodge in September.) While praising Lodge for having given the treaty its only possible chance for success, Root, in December, advised compromising on "face-saving modification" not involving "the sacrifice of essential substance."[31] A compromise on reservations would establish the sincerity of the Republican party, to Root an objective more important than the mere success or failure of the League.

Lodge rejected Root's proposals altogether. They were not advisable or expedient. "Verbal changes," he declared, "to save Democrats' faces are silly." The Republican party position was secure; the Treaty would have passed at any time that the President had accepted the reservations. Wilson, and Wilson alone, was responsible for the defeat of the Treaty. If he persisted in rejecting reservations, Lodge, feeling sure of victory, would be happy to carry the issue into the next election.[32]

By the end of December Lodge was publicly favorable to compromise. But this seeming change of heart was no more than a political maneuver. As Lodge explained to the irreconcilable Beveridge, "It would have been a mistake for me to have taken the attitude that we would not even consider modifications. We could not have afforded to say that. . . ." Indeed, Lodge's position could scarcely have been more steadfast. He was never willing to compromise on Article Ten; he was determined to have reservations. Wilson, it was obvious, would not compromise on Article Ten and would not, Lodge thought, accept any reservations. The President, Lodge wrote, was in no physical condition to consider reservations and his "inability to carry on the Government is now clear. . . ."[33]

Lodge accordingly agreed to work with a seven-man Bi-Partisan Committee, formed about the middle of January, which sought for two weeks to reach a compromise. At the time these meetings began, Lodge wrote that Article Ten was "the crucial point." If the conference broke up without reaching an agreement, the break "should be on Article 10."[34] Lodge would have been consistent in holding to an uncompromising stand. Contemporary accounts, however, picture Lodge and Simmons on the point of reaching agreement on a reservation to Article Ten. At this critical moment Lodge was called from the meeting. Confronted by Borah, Knox, Johnson, and other irreconcilables, he was told that compromise would mean the end of party unity. Bowing to the inevitable, Lodge announced on January 26 that there could be no compromise on Article Ten or the Monroe Doctrine.[35]

Meanwhile, Hitchcock on January 22 sent the Simmons reservation on Article Ten to Wilson. The President replied on January 26, the same day Lodge rejected the compromise, that he would not willingly accept the Simmons reservation. The substance was satisfactory to him, but he felt the form unfortunate. A reservation stating that the United

States assumes no obligation under such and such an article "unless or except" Wilson felt would "chill our relationship with the nations with which we expect to be associated." It was of paramount importance that the United States should not create the impression of trying to escape an obligation. Wilson was willing, however, to seek compromise on the basis of the reservations he had earlier given Hitchcock.[36]

These reservations were not actually used in the Senate debate. But several days after getting Wilson's letter, Hitchcock, still seeking agreement, asked Lodge if he would accept, as a basis of compromise, the Taft reservation to Article Ten. It stated: "The United States declines to assume any legal or binding obligation to preserve the territorial integrity or political independence of any other country under the provisions of Article 10 or to employ the military or naval forces of the United States under any article of the treaty for any purpose; but the Congress, which under the Constitution has the sole power in the premises, will consider and decide what moral obligation, if any, under the circumstances of any particular case, when it arises, should move the United States in the interest of world peace and justice to take action therein and will provide accordingly." This reservation actually met all of the requirements that Lodge had set forth only two days earlier. Now he refused to consider the Taft reservation as a basis of compromise and insisted that his original reservation to Article Ten be used. Hitchcock blamed Lodge's reversal of opinion on the irreconcilables and asserted bitterly that compromise on both Article Ten and the Monroe Doctrine reservations had been within sight. Probably Hitchcock was overly influenced by wishful thinking. Lodge was willing to accept changes in the phraseology of his reservation to Article Ten, and this was enough to terrify the irreconcilables, but he was not willing to accept a moral obligation to act. Even if Lodge's convictions had been otherwise, it would have been folly as a party leader to test, in an election year, the determination of irreconcilable Republicans to 'have their way or bolt the party.

The Bi-Partisan Committee broke down completely by the end of January. However, the spirit of compromise was not dead. On February 9 the Senate formally voted to reconsider the Treaty and the futile process of seeking agreement began again. Results were encouraging for a time. Eight of the fourteen Lodge reservations were adopted or revised by March 7. Still no progress had been achieved on the reservation to Article Ten, although Hitchcock showed himself anxious to reach agreement. The various versions of the reservation were brought close together, but no final agreement could be achieved.

The last move toward compromise on Article Ten was initiated in March by Democratic Senator Simmons with the support of Republican Senator Jim Watson and with Lodge's approval. Wilson, however, refused to see Simmons and discuss the reservation.[37] Apparently the President had given up what slight hope he had entertained for Senate ratification of the Treaty. He looked to the people to vindicate him with a Democratic victory at the polls in November. By letter to Hitchcock, March 8, Wilson denounced any attempt to devitalize or nullify Article Ten, "the essence of Americanism," by any reservations compromising its moral obligation.

To some the Senate debate on Article Ten was nothing more than empty sound and fury. Such experts in international law as Root and Leon Bourgeois of France asserted that Article Ten was not vital to the operation of the League. David Hunter Miller could see no real issue in the controversy over reservations. With or without the reservations the Covenant was virtually the same thing. In a legal sense these experts were correct. Mere legal compliance with a Covenant would not carry weight in world affairs. Article Ten represented the willingness of a nation to dedicate itself to insuring peace. Lodge declared that the reservations to Article Ten were specifically designed to free the United States of any obligation to preserve world peace. The reservations in essence if not in letter denied the whole theory of collective security.

To Wilson the Senate debate was vital. He never ceased to feel that Article Ten was the "very heart and life" of the League Covenant. "Any League of Nations," he declared, "which does not guarantee as a matter of incontestable right the political independence and integrity of its members might be hardly more than a futile scrap of paper." Rejecting or weakening Article Ten, the President added, "would mark us as desiring to return to the old world of jealous rivalry and misunderstandings from which our gallant soldiers have rescued us. . . . If America has awakened, as the rest of the world has, to the vision of a new day in which the mistakes of the past are to be corrected, it will welcome the opportunity to share the responsibilities of Article X."[38]

CHAPTER VIII

The Fight Centers on Article X

In retrospect it is clear that America's final rejection of Article Ten, as well as the balance of the League of Nations Covenant, came November 2, 1920, with the landslide election of Harding to the presidency. It is generally held, however, that this decision was not the result of a conscious choice by the voters; that it was not the "solemn referendum" that Wilson hoped it would be. The decision really came during the next four years as the victorious Republican administration equivocated and evaded the issue of world organization until popular interest became apathetic. Of course the presidential election, as always, involved many conflicting issues of domestic politics, making it impossible to say with certainty that a vote for Harding was a vote against the League. For one thing, if the League had been considered the paramount issue, it is argued, Harding's speeches were too indefinite to show where he stood. For another, the voters, bored with eighteen months of debate, were indifferent to the League as a campaign issue.

Further confusion resulted from attempts to determine the actual ability of the candidates to carry out in terms of practical politics their campaign promises. Assuming that Harding was opposed to the League, it was argued that he would be forced to accept it after election in order to conciliate the Hughes-Root-Taft wing of the party. Cox, although for the Wilson League, could never as President drive it through a Senate in which more than a third opposed Article Ten. His election would mean nothing more than a continuation of the stalemate between President and Senate.

There is much truth in these generalizations. Yet, it is true also that the contemporary press felt the League was the major issue of the election. The pro-League *New York*

Times said in October that "the people are deeply interested in the League of Nations. . . . The issue, the managers say, is now squarely before the people in the referendum on November 2. The election of Cox means a League of Nations acceptable to President Wilson, and Republican success apparently precludes American participation in the League." Such anti-League papers as the *New York American* and the *Chicago Tribune* also declared in October that "the issue at this election is whether we are going into the Wilson Covenant or staying out."[1]

Both candidates stressed the League issue throughout the campaign, with increasing emphasis as election day neared. Taft, for example, complained late in October that Cox talked about nothing but the League, using it as a cloak to hide the many shortcomings of the Wilson administration in domestic politics.[2] In his final speech of the campaign Cox sought to reduce the issues to one—the League. Harding closed his speaking with the declaration that the Republicans said No and the Democrats said Yes to entering the League and assuming the obligations of Article Ten.[3]

From the amorphous oratory of the campaign emerged startlingly stark and definite opinions on Article Ten. This one of the Covenant's twenty-six Articles was singled out and condemned, for reasons of political expediency as well as principle, by all important factions of the Republican party. It was denounced with a finality seldom employed in elections except to excoriate the prevalence of sin in the opposing administration.

There was a general recognition of vast difference between a League with Article Ten and a League without that provision, the difference being between terminating traditional policies of non-entanglement and continuing those policies, between unending responsible involvement in European politics and complete freedom of choice in foreign policy. The positive qualities of a League without Article Ten were not defined during the campaign, but the negative features of the mutual guarantee were made unmistakably clear.

Harding, for all of his skillful obfuscation of issues, with the hearty approval of the irreconcilables spoke out clearly against the mutual guarantee. The so-called pro-League wing

of the Republican party publicly and emphatically declared
its rejection of Article Ten in the widely published Appeal of
the Thirty-One. This rejection was made even more final
when two of the faction's most respected and best informed
leaders, Root and Hughes, strongly condemned Article Ten
many times in speeches during the closing days of the
campaign.

In the Democratic camp there was more of a struggle over
the Article. Cox and Roosevelt sought to stand by Wilson's
program for immediate ratification without crippling reservations. But the party platform did not preclude reservations
making American obligations clearer and more specific. As
the campaign neared its end, Cox placed more and more
emphasis on this escape clause, giving the impression that
he would accept sweeping changes to Article Ten. Alarmed
Republicans feared he would soon run on their platform.
Certainly it was not clear that a vote for Cox in November
was a vote for an unreserved and unmodified Article Ten.

The Republican party at its National Convention had
called once again on the "shrewd mind and cunning hand"
of Elihu Root to frame a statement on the League in general
on which its friends and enemies within the party could unite.
Despite Root's magnificent effort to please all factions the
battle for control of the candidate continued. The campaign
speeches of Harding indicated a movement away from the
League and toward a wholly different organization desig-
nated as an association of nations. Conceived in August with
the aid of George Harvey and Richard Washburn Child, the
association of nations drew the conflicting statements of
Harding into a complicated and ambiguous plan for international cooperation designed as a straddle enabling Harding to placate the irreconcilables, who wanted no league,
and the liberals, who wished to join the League. In short,
he promised at this time to work with the "best minds" in the
country after his election in order to establish "a society
of free nations . . . so organized as to make attainment of
peace a reasonable possibility."[4] Later in the campaign Harding was pushed into the irreconcilable camp to keep Brandegee and Johnson from bolting the party. Harding soon
realized that "This issue . . . does not present to the American people the question whether they shall favor some form

of association among the nations for the purpose of preserving international peace, but whether they favor the
particular League proposed by President Wilson. . . . The
obligations are clear enough and specific enough. I oppose
the League not because I fail to understand . . . 'What we
are being let in for,' but because I believe I understand precisely 'what we are being let in for.'

"I do not want to clarify these obligations; I want to
turn my back on them. It is not interpretation but rejection,
that I am seeking. My position is that the present league
strikes a deadly blow at our constitutional integrity and
surrenders to a dangerous extent our independence of
action. . . .

"The issue therefore is clear. I understand the position
of the Democratic candidate and he understands mine. . . .
It is that he favors going into the Paris League and I favor
staying out. . . . We shall have an association of nations
for the promotion of international peace, but one which shall
so definitely safeguard our sovereignty and recognize our ultimate and unmortgaged freedom of action. . . . that it will have
back of it the united support of the American people."[5]

On Article Ten Harding was even more clear and
specific. He described Article Ten as "not only the most
dangerous provision in the Covenant, but, in its sinister possibilities, it is the most dangerous proposition ever presented
to the American people." With words of "utmost pre-
cision" the Article bound America to "an obligation which
under certain easily foreseeable circumstances will require the
use of armed forces. It is true that the Constitution invests
Congress with the sole power to declare war, but if war shall
become necessary in order to fulfill this or any other treaty
provision Congress must either declare war or repudiate
the obligation. Let no one be deceived; the choice would
be between two things—war and dishonor."[6] Nevertheless,
Harding favored a league provided the United States was
required to act only in accord with the "test of righteousness" and assume no other obligation. A few days later,
Harding asserted that Article Ten was indeed the "heart
of the League" as Wilson had asserted. "I know it is
the heart of the League,—the steel heart, hidden beneath
a coat of mail. Article 10 creates a world government,

puts America in alliance with four great powers to rule the world by force of arms and commits America to give her sons for all the battlefields of the Old World."[7]

Republican supporters of the League found that Harding's steady drift toward its rejection made it difficult for them to harmonize ideals with political loyalties. Some were able to rationalize their position. Taft achieved this feat by accepting two assumptions. The first and most important was that he had overestimated the importance of Article Ten. Harding, Taft reasoned in his second assumption, must be a better friend of peace than Wilson. Despite Harding's campaign speeches he would take the nation into the League with reservations once the election was over. Then, too, Harding was a Republican.[8] Irreconcilables, like Hiram Johnson, were little impressed with the Taft promise of a league. The California Senator asserted that "Taft can save his face so long as he doesn't save his League."[9]

For many Republicans Harding's attacks on the League and Taft's assurances that all was well were alike unsatisfactory. Some of them, under the leadership of Professor Irvine Fisher, organized the pro-League Independents and called for Republicans who favored the League to vote for Cox. This movement attracted membership from the "best element" of the Republican party.[10] Others of this group who remained loyal to the party found their position more and more disagreeable as Harding took a stronger position against the League.

Early in October the Democrats launched a campaign to have the text of the Covenant published as widely as possible. The Chairman of the Democratic National Committee, George White, asked Will Hays to enlist the cooperation of Republican newspapers for such a program "in the interest of truth which the righteous certainly have no reason to fear. . . ."[11] The Republican party was cool to the suggestion. At the same time the party leadership did not wish to be pushed to a definite position against the League. To counteract the reluctance to take a stand, Hays enlisted once again the services of Elihu Root. They raised, with the aid of Jacob Gould Schurman, Paul D. Cravath, and George Wickersham, a standard to which pro-League Republicans might rally. To add greater luster their argument was signed by thirty-one leading Republicans, including "seventeen college presidents and executives."[12]

The Appeal of the Thirty-One (the name afterwards given the document) was remarkable even as campaign literature. It was accepted as a firm approval "for the League of Nations in the form in which it had been endorsed by the League to Enforce Peace," to quote Hays.[13] Yet nowhere in the document was any such statement made; "the" League was referred to only as "the proposed agreement." While support for "a" league was offered, the closest approach to endorsement of "the" League was the statement: "We therefore believe that we can effectively advance the cause of international co-operation to promote peace by supporting Mr. Harding. . . ."

So vague was the actual text that it inspired many interpretations. The *New York Times*, for example, deduced that the proposal advocated taking the best features from the League Covenant and combining them with Root's plan for an international court. The finished creation, it was inferred, would be an entirely new organization, an association of nations.[14]

Even if the signees had advocated adherence to the League of Nations, there was little possibility that they could have executed their pledge. As President H. N. McCracken of Vassar said in refusing to sign the appeal, "The names of those signing it will not in my opinion have influence on Senator Harding's foreign policy after the election."[15]

All of this might have been apparent to any other careful reader of the Appeal. But there were few careful readers, and there were many voters who wanted to be assured that they could support the League and Harding. The statement was accepted by the public as a full endorsement of a modified League by men who would make the foreign policy of the Republican administration. Chairman Hays, on the one hand, and candidate Cox, on the other, agreed that the Appeal influenced thousands of wavering Republicans to vote for Harding.[16]

The change of votes did not decide the election by any means. The Appeal, however, was especially significant in the history of Article Ten. For all of its vagueness as to the League of Nations, the Appeal was remarkably clear and specific in its renunciation of Article Ten. It called in unequivocal language for the elimination of Article Ten from any peace plan considered by the United States and the establishment of a legal tribunal resting on the enforcing power of public opinion.

The Thirty-one acknowledged that Wilson believed Article Ten to be the "heart of the League." They then attacked the Article with the same arguments the most irreconcilable Senate opponents had employed. Article Ten, the statement asserted, obligated all members "to go to war whenever war may be necessary to preserve the territorial integrity or political independence of any member of the League against external aggression." The Thirty-one recommended "that the true course to bring Americans into an effective league to preserve peace is not by insisting with Mr. Cox upon the acceptance of such a provision as Article X . . . but by frankly calling upon the other nations to agree to changes in the proposed agreement which will obviate this vital objection." To accomplish this aim "we can look only to the Republican Party and its candidate; the Democratic Party and Mr. Cox are not bound to follow it."[17]

Actually, the statement did little to clarify and much to confuse the issue at the time. It did help create the impression (as Root, its principal author, had hoped) that the real issue was the Wilson League, based on force, versus an "Americanized" league, based on law. Furthermore, Root philosophized, leagues in the popular mind were synonymous with peace, and so it was expedient for Republicans during the campaign to advocate some sort of league in order to attract the vote of "clergymen, women, and other good people."[18]

Shortly after the Appeal, Root made in Carnegie Hall on October 18 his only speech of the campaign. In an unreserved attack on Article Ten he declared that it was no part of the main scheme of the League of Nations and actually "inconsistent with the purpose and spirit of the League." Article Ten was in fact nothing more than "an alliance to enforce perpetually through the operations of the League the decisions of Mr. Wilson and his associates in the year 1919." It would preserve forever the inequities of the Treaty of Versailles. The language of power but not of progress spoken by Article Ten was in "negation of the opinions held by the wisest, most experienced, and most devoted men who have labored in all civilized countries for generations to advance the cause of peace." A league might be useful provided it was shorn of any obligations to employ force, moral or physical, on behalf of the Treaty of Versailles. Although Root honestly opposed the use of force as an instrument of peace, he went in this speech beyond the bounds of fairness and truth in his condemnation of Article Ten. He was guilty, as Charles Eliot charged, of "extraordinary partisanship."[19]

Another prominent signer of the Appeal of the Thirty-one, Charles Evans Hughes, was more explicit in condemning Article Ten. He asserted, in a speech in New Haven, October 23: "We desire to have the obligation of Article X nullified, for it has no place in a proper covenant for an association of nations to promote peace." In great detail Hughes explained that Wilson in his interpretative reservations to Article Ten had never touched this central issue—America's obligation to act. Wilson insisted upon Article Ten "because it does impose an obligation and because he desires the United States to rest under that obligation." That was why Wilson would not accept the Lodge reservation, for the point of that reservation, declared Hughes, "is that it denies the obligation itself." Cox, too, in announcing his willingness to accept modifications to Article Ten was not prepared to nullify the obligation it imposed. The real and only issue of the campaign, Hughes insisted, was Article Ten. The Republicans were against "the obligation as one which we cannot assume in accordance with the principles of our institutions." Hughes was completely honest and consistent in his abhorrence to the obligations of Article Ten, as he was to demonstrate so many times during the next four years as secretary of state. It is difficult to argue that he did not read the sentiment of the American people with great accuracy.[20]

In a political campaign ideas of great impact must be expressed in simple terms. The election was a vote for peace or war, said the *New York Times*. Candidate Cox declared that it was a simple question of "the gospel of Cain against the gospel of Christ." Thus the League meant peace;

a vote against it meant war.[21] But this easily comprehended idea was clouded by the Republican attack on Article Ten. A league meant peace; Article Ten meant war. The force of this argument had impressed many Democrats—so many in fact that the party platform was not the unreserved endorsement for the League that Wilson wished, but was tempered by the agreement to accept helpful reservations. Early in October, Governor Cox announced that he favored a reservation to Article Ten stating that the United States would not assume an obligation to defend other members of the League "unless approved and authorized by Congress in each case." Such a change could mean that the moral force of the guarantee against aggression would be seriously impaired if not completely eliminated. Cox gave no specific interpretation of the reservation, but he did deny publicly Root's charge that he would "insist upon the Treaty just as Mr. Wilson negotiated it." He went on to say, "I will accept reservations that will clarify, that will be helpful, that will reassure the American people, and that as a matter of good faith will clearly state to our associates in the League that Congress and Congress alone has the right to declare war, and that our Constitution sets up limits in legislation or treaty-making beyond which we can not go."[22] Any reservations from any source, Cox added, would be carefully considered provided they were proffered in the spirit of sincerity and helpfulness. If elected he promised to sit down and consider the League with the members of the Senate, with Wilson, with Root, with Taft, and with all other sincere friends of the Treaty.

These were campaign statements and might mean much or little. Generally they were interpreted as meaning that Cox was weakening his advocacy of Article Ten. The *New York Times* expressed some surprise that Wilson was willing to endorse Cox's work in a letter published just before the election.[23] Elsewhere Cox's advocacy of the League was denounced as uninformed and ineffectual.[24] The *New Republic* declared Article Ten to be dead even before the election. Cox had repudiated it and no Republican faction favored the Article.[25]

There was poignant symbolism in Wilson's first speech in over a year, delivered at the close of the campaign. Seated in a wheel chair and speaking in a voice barely audible, Wilson declared that unless Article Ten was honored, the League would be virtually worthless. Article Ten, he continued, assured the world that a future aggressor would not run rampant as Germany had done in 1914. It was "the specific redemption of the pledge which the free governments of the world gave to their people when they entered the war."[26] In America. however, the pledge had been repudiated even before the speech was made. The revolution in American foreign policy, like its leader, was mortally ill. Few who went to the polls heeded the message of the broken old man in the White House.

Contemporary observers were not all willing to accept the verdict of the *Nation* that the discussions on the League during the campaign were "almost 100 per cent flapdoodle." The issue, noted the *Literary Digest,* was one "that would not down" and "it is upon Article X that the fight centers at the last." It was "the pith of the controversy." The pro-League *Philadelphia Public Ledger,* even before the election, concluded that the American people would not accept a covenant containing Article Ten. Only "an exceedingly poor student of political psychology" would cherish any hope that Article Ten could be put through the Senate in the next two years.[27] The *New Republic* agreed but believed that "behind the Senate Republicans there was a profound popular instinct against the character of the peace," and an unwillingness to enforce the Treaty of Versailles by force of arms. This opinion was confirmed to the satisfaction of the editor by the results of the election.[28] The people were overwhelmingly against Article Ten.[29]

The result of the election was, no doubt, too one-sided to be ascribed to any one cause more definite than "a mighty wave of protest." As for the League, the results frequently were interpreted to suit the hopes of the interpreter. Hiram Johnson, on the one hand, was sure the issue in the election had been the League and "no amount of sophistry or pretense" could obscure the fact that "the menacing, dangerous, and entangling league has been emphatically and overwhelmingly repudiated."[30] Herbert Hoover, on the other hand, asserted that "the vote as a whole" was "distinctly in favor of the participation of the United States in some form of interna-

tional agreement for the maintenance of peace."[31] To a
marked degree the real problem was simply one of semantics.
Judging by the campaign statements and considering the
record of events during the next two decades, it is safe
to say that the people had repudiated Article Ten. Taft
probably outlined in his post-election statement the most
advanced type of international organization that Americans
would have accepted. The organization, which he was sure
Harding would establish soon, would center "around an
international court, with teeth in it." Article Ten "of course,
must be eliminated if the United States is to enter a league."
Otherwise the ground-plan, or organization, of the present
League, improved by amendments, would fulfill Harding's
aim.[32]

The fight in 1920 centered on Article Ten and it was
consciously and emphatically eliminated from any plans for
American participation in international organizations. The
one theory on which Wilson had built his whole League
program was dead. The idea of a league still had popular
appeal but only to the degree that commitments and obligations were eliminated. The Wilson League was dead in the
United States. What the Harding association of nations
could do with the United States as a free agent whose "only
interest and commitment would be to the peace of the world"
remained to be seen.

CHAPTER IX

Referendum for Isolation

DURING the campaign of 1920 all except the most irreconcilable critics of the League tempered their attacks with the promise of an equally effective but vastly less demanding peace organization. Shrewd politicians surveyed the climate of opinion and concluded that in the public mind the terms league and peace were inseparable. Therefore it was expedient to demand "a league but not this one." To this end the obliging Harding promised, from time to time and in a vague and general way, to establish an association of nations that could foster peace without impairing American sovereignty. The one-sided election returns, however, indicated that the appeal of the League was less compelling than anticipated. Harding declared immediately that the League of Nations was "deceased."[1] Certainly a league centered on the ideal of Article Ten was dead and in the light of later events, Harding might have broadened his statement to include any type of league.

There were, it is true, a number of determined and articulate champions of the League for two decades after its defeat. Few were popular leaders who commanded the loyalty of a significant and unified body of public opinion. Moreover, advocates of an international organization in the United States were never able, in the ensuing years, to agree on the place of military force in the peace movement. There was no grass roots demand for a league and, in fact, no foundation for such a movement.

Wilson pitched the call to arms in 1917 on a plane of high idealism. When he sought to redeem his promises to end war by his program at the peace table, his followers became disillusioned, confused, and angry at the high cost of a better world. Possibly Wilson would have been on sounder ground by reducing war and peace aims to the realistic terms of national interest. In any event, the relation of American security to an effective league was not demonstrated in such a way as to capture the public imagination. The new departure in American foreign policy called for by Article Ten was in the nature of a palace revolution that never extended to the people. Or perhaps it would be more accurate to say it did not go beyond the vision and voice of one lonely prophet crying in the wilderness.

These facts became increasingly clear to Republican party leaders after the election. In time they became somewhat embarrassed by the pledge to establish an association of nations. It became apparent that their procrastination in executing this pledge would never end.

The trend toward ignoring the pledge, however, was not apparent at first. So interested a spectator as Senator Borah feared, immediately following the election, that Hughes, Root, and their followers would insist on framing up "some kind of League" for the Republican party to support.[2] The press and the public assumed that Harding would attempt to carry out his campaign pledge for international cooperation by proposing an association of nations freed of the obligations of an Article Ten.[3] Harding, it seemed for a time, set himself to this task. Relinquishing his seat in the Senate he retired to his home in Marion, Ohio. During the following two weeks he held consultations on foreign affairs at his home with a number of Republican leaders.[4]

One of the first visitors was Charles Evans Hughes, rumored to be a possible choice for a cabinet post, who held, so it was reported, a two-hour discussion with the President-elect on international affairs. It was thought that they discussed the League of Nations and the association of nations.[5] Harding's interest in the association of nations was definitely confirmed at a later meeting with George Harvey, an inveterate foe of the League and author of many of Harding's equivocal campaign speeches on that subject. Harvey was wholeheartedly in favor of an association of nations in which no nation could declare war without a popular referendum.[6]

In view of Harding's indebtedness to and sympathy with the Senate, his interview with the irreconcilable Senator Albert B. Fall was of great significance. Fall asserted that the irreconcilable opponents of the League were in favor of some sort of association of nations. In explaining his view Senator Fall declared in a statement typical of the opinion of the Senate: "I was an irreconcilable and I still am. I believe we owe a duty to the other peoples of the world, but I always have thought we could do it without surrendering any part of our sovereignty." The irreconcilables, he continued, wanted peace and recognized that international cooperation was necessary to maintain it. They did not believe, however, that cooperation should be carried to the extent of sacrificing American rights and American sovereignty.[7]

Harding's views seemed to be taking form when he told another distinguished visitor, Nicholas Murray Butler, that the American people had rejected a league and wanted an association of nations. Butler did not agree. He urged the President-elect to take the nation into a modified league. If this course was impossible, Butler favored, as the next best solution, a conference, preferably at Washington, to clear up the remaining problems left by the war and to launch an association of nations.[8]

Many other notables conferred with Harding during the ensuing days. While no definite details of the interviews were made public, the general belief was that the plans discussed included an association of nations. There appeared to be general agreement in favor of such an association among all Republican leaders, including many irreconcilables in the Senate.

One dissenter was Senator Borah. Even though he did not relax his campaign, Borah felt by January, 1921, that there would be no definite program for a league or for an association. Harding would wait until he got into office to act. Then the whole plan would be one of procrastination and postponement. A great deal of time would be consumed in drafting plans for an association of nations and infinite delay would accompany the efforts to put it into practice.[9]

The Senator was not worried when Harding, early in the year, announced, in an interview with Jacob Gould Schurman, that the basic problem in policy was the establishment of the association of nations to work for disarmament, codify international law, establish a world court, and organize world

conferences for the settlement of disputes beyond the scope
of international law.[10] Subsequently, this policy, as outlined
to Schurman, was befogged by a number of conflicting
reports.

The consistent failure to define a policy increased popular
interest as to what the President might say on foreign affairs
in his inaugural address. Here, in keeping with his campaign
promises, he rejected Article Ten, postulating his policy on
complete independence for the United States in international
relations. He declared that America would never become
a party to any military alliance or "enter into political
commitments nor assume any economic obligations or subject
our decisions to any other than our own authority." Even
more specific were the President's statements that "the
League Covenant can have no sanction by us," and that
the policy of independent action was "patriotic adherence
to the things that made us what we are."

America, however, stood ready to associate itself with the
countries of the world in conferences "to suggest plans for
arbitration and the establishment of a world court," and to
make offensive war so hateful that those who resorted to it
would stand "as outlaws before the bar of civilization." This
cooperation would not violate the basic postulate of unfettered independence, for "every commitment must be made in
the exercise of our national sovereignty."[11]

The public, because of Harding's statements of policy
early in the year, had expected an association to be announced in his inaugural. Neither then nor in the months
immediately following did the administration launch an
association. Many interpreted this silence, nevertheless, as
evidence that the President had not altered his original policy
and that he still planned to carry out his campaign promise
for an association of nations. Surveys of opinion indicated a
demand for him to fulfill his pledge to establish a world
organization.

Possibly Harding, and certainly some of his advisors,
thought the association might be organized at the Washington
Conference scheduled for the fall of 1921. Charles D. Hilles
in August wrote a confidential letter to the President suggesting that the Conference be considered a part of his
larger plan for the association of nations.[12] Early in Septem-

ber, Chandler P. Anderson proposed "to work out" for the State Department "the framework of an association of nations as an agency for what might be called international administrative rather than executive action." Hughes after a month replied that the policy regarding the association of nations was very indefinite and would not be considered until the right moment presented itself. Anderson's offer was welcomed, however, and he was told to proceed with developing a definite basis for an association of nations.[13] Incidentally, the statement by Hughes was made only two weeks before the opening of the Conference at a time when other major policies had been reduced to definite form.

Speculation that the real purpose of the Conference was to launch the association was not confined to the United States. Members of the League of Nations became apprehensive over the possible establishment of a rival organization at the Washington Conference. The United States, it was suggested, planned to kill the League of Nations and establish a thoroughly "American" association.[14]

As the time for the opening of the Conference approached, many American citizens who were hopeful that an association of nations would be established had reason to be encouraged. They interpreted Secretary Hughes' statement in his opening speech that the Washington Conference was bent upon taking definite action to meet the problems before it to mean the establishment of an association. Surveys of the press showed that the public expected daily the announcement of a plan for the establishment of an association of nations.[15] The popular assumption appeared to be justified when Harding began to "hint" that the Washington Conference was to be the foundation of a larger association of nations, the first of a series of conferences. These meetings, including all nations, would be held whenever a crisis arose. The *New York Times* was enthusiastic: "Germ of New 'Association' Seen in Suggested Annual Meetings." This was a development, it declared, dwarfing all other matters taken up by the Conference.[16]

Though Harding's proposal remained indefinite in form it created a mild sensation. It was discussed in Congress and won the unofficial approval of the pro-League senators and enough additional support to secure a majority. Even at this elementary stage, however, the proposal aroused the ire and opposition of the anti-League senators. The assault was led by Senator Borah, inveterate foe of "any international league, association, combination, or alliance of any kind"— even the association of nations mentioned by Harding during the most critical days of the presidential campaign.

In a speech that attracted headlines over the nation, Borah reminded the President that any such plan as he was reported to have in mind must have the consent of the Senate. The new proposal, said Borah, was even more dangerous than the League. The old League was defined in its powers, while the new association of nations called for nothing but "a conclave of diplomats, sitting behind closed doors with nothing to direct or limit their powers save their own will and discretion." Furthermore, no useful purpose could be served by the creation of a new organization to do the same work done by the League. Finally, said Borah, "If we are going into Europe we ought to go in. If we are not, we ought not to be handing her a new league every ninety days."[17]

It was reported that the irreconcilables threatened Harding. In any event he suddenly decided to become more cautious in launching his plan. He seemed to realize that his "hint" had gone too far for a very influential part of American opinion. Indeed he faced an active revolt. The President subsequently denied that he had approached foreign delegates or members of the American delegation on the matter of establishing an association, or broached the subject to the American delegation at any time.

Some papers insisted that Harding's plan was in response to a public trend. Americans, it was argued, were beginning to realize that "the most emphatic result of the conference so far has been to make evident that though conferences can initiate proposals, only alliances or world associations can carry them to effective conclusions and give them continuous operation."[18] The surveys of public opinion, which the Committee on General Information conducted, showed that the number of organizations over the country favoring an association was gradually increasing.[19] Typical of the optimism shown in the press was the *New York Tribune's* opinion that "the Association of Nations, not yet achieved, seems about to be realized." This optimism was unfounded. Harding let the association of nations die, although the press refused to bury it.

The finality of the association's defeat and with it the last feeble hope for any American approval of collective security was not realized by the internationalists, who continued to be optimistic and determined. One of these who had signed the Appeal of the Thirty-one, President A. Lawrence Lowell of Harvard University, wrote Hughes in 1922 urging that the administration carry the association through to completion.[20] Hughes, in a blunt reply, made it plain that the administration had no intention of executing such plans. "We have been dealing with matters in a practical way and have accomplished a great deal. If there are those who think that they should renew a barren controversy, that is their right. Nothing good will come of it, and very likely it will stand in the way of much that might otherwise be accomplished." The Secretary added that the real difficulty was not in a lack of machinery "but the attitude and opinion of peoples." Furthermore, Hughes, it appeared, was tired of hearing such pleas. "The President does not think, and I entirely agree with him, that he should refer again, at this time to his desire for an Association of Nations. . . ."[21] These statements were conclusive, but they were not made public.

Nor were they accepted by Lowell. He felt that his pledge to establish a league as a signer of the Appeal of the Thirty-one had not been discharged by the Republican administration. In May of 1923 he arranged a dinner meeting in New York City of those persons who had signed the Appeal. He hoped that a declaration might be drawn calling on the administration to carry out its solemn pledge to establish an association of nations. The meeting brought from Harding a denial that he had promised an association of nations or even approved the Appeal of the Thirty-one. Lowell, a few days later, answered the President in a speech in Washington and quoted passage after passage from Harding's campaign speeches defining the issue to be the League as opposed to a modified league. The standard was raised, but only one of the thirty that stood with Lowell in October, 1920, supported him in May of 1923.[22] The League was dead. More significantly, the infinitely more vapid association of nations, with no hint of an Article Ten, no obligations, and no commitments, was dead also.

Indeed, in the United States after 1920 there was a great, an apparently almost universal, revulsion against war but no enthusiasm for employing international coercion to enforce peace. A peace plan typical of the times was presented by Republican Senator Porter J. McCumber, once a strong advocate of the League and Article Ten. He proposed an association of nations, resting "entirely upon the sacred national honor of each Government, supported by an informed public conscience that will not brook any international injustice."[23]

More explicit was Senator Borah. He clearly expressed the opinion in 1921 of many senators: "One of the revolting monstrosities born of the war, the legitimate offspring of secret diplomacy and violence, is the absurd, iniquitous belief that you can only have peace through martial means—that force is the only power on earth with which to govern men. I denounce the hideous, diabolical idea, and I insist that this Government ought to be counted against all plans, all treaties, all programs, all policies based on this demoniacal belief." Again he declared that there had been two thousand years of the worship of force. He asked: "What are the fruits? If anyone is familiar with the vernacular of Hell, let him undertake to paint the picture. Human tongue is inadequate to the task."[24]

Borah, and others, advanced a doctrine of the two hemispheres in relation to the use of force. The essence of all European plans for preserving peace had been employment of military sanctions—creation in a new form of the old system of alliances. The American system stood on the acceptance of moral sanctions, trusting in the conscience of nations to make it operative.

Secretary Hughes at the Washington Conference, 1921-1922, sought to translate rejection of binding obligations by the American people into sound policy. To such an end he drafted treaties incorporating none but moral obligations and specifically denying commitments.

Even so in the debates of the Washington Conference on the treaties a determination to abjure cooperative action was restated again and again by the Senate. Such men as James

Reed, Johnson, and Borah saw in Article Two of the Four-Power Treaty, providing for consultation to follow the failure to settle differences through diplomatic channels, the same legal and moral obligations provided by Article Ten of the League Covenant. These obligations and consequent dangers remained even though Hughes and Harding had sought to eliminate them. Harding in presenting the treaties to the Senate declared that "The conclusions reached and the covenants written neither require nor contemplate compulsive measures against any power in the world, signatory or nonsignatory. The offerings are free will; the conscience is that of world-opinion; the observance is a matter of national honor. . . . There are mutual and essential interests affecting the welfare and peace of all nations, and they can not be promoted by force." Lest some obtuse senator should fail to get his message, Harding specified that the treaty contained "no commitment to armed force, no alliance, no written or moral obligation to join in defense, no expressed or implied commitment to arrive at any agreement except in accordance with constitutional methods." Thus the force of the treaty rested alone on "moral warnings" and the "focus of world opinion on a given controversy."[25]

The Senate, skeptical of this and later assurances by the administration that no obligations were involved, incorporated Harding's pledge in the Brandegee reservation to the Four-Power Treaty. The largest vote given any treaty or proposed reservation in the Senate was the 93 to 0 vote of confidence given the Brandegee reservation.[26]

These measures might be dismissed as an effort to obstruct the treaties. Yet even those defending the Four-Power Treaty in the Senate did not endorse collective military force or favor the assumption of obligations or commitments. Their defense was negative. There was little possibility that action would be needed, they insisted; the treaty related to an area in which future trouble was unlikely to develop. If controversy did arise, the treaty called for consultation but not for action.

. . . .

By what margin had the opposition to the League of Nations triumphed? Advocates argued that the League failed by the margin of the handful of votes needed to gain a two-

thirds majority. "A little group of willful men," to use
Wilson's expression in another connection, had defied the
wishes of the majority of the American people and kept the
United States from joining the League. Thus shorn of its
strongest member, the League never had any real chance for
success. And the argument can be extended into claiming that
the blame for the catastrophe of the Second World War
can be attributed to a few stubborn American senators.

In the perspective of time, this charge appears to be exaggerated. Article Ten was the heart of the League, of the
system of collective security. America was not, however,
ready to take this long step toward international cooperation into a league of mutual guarantee. Wilson's advisors
within his own party opposed it. The responsible leadership
as well as the irresponsible elements of the Republican party
opposed Article Ten. While the people, it may be argued,
favored the League by an overwhelming majority, few ever
read the text of the Covenant and, far from assuming new
obligations, they hoped by joining a league to end all problems in international affairs. They did not want to assume
commitments. The Republicans after 1921 were unwilling,
and perhaps unable, to launch an association of nations, even
without any binding obligations. Only when assured many
times over that no obligation was involved did the United
States government accept even the negative guarantee of the
Kellogg-Briand Pact. Thus the weight of tradition as it had
developed before the League debate and as it continued to
grow for almost two decades afterwards tends to show
that there was really very little chance the United States
would adopt the League and only a slight possibility that its
obligations would have been carried out in good faith.

It was his confident belief that the people, as distinguished
from their political leaders, were determined to have a League
of Nations that prompted Wilson to carry the issue into the
1920 presidential campaign. His disappointment when the
election ended in defeat was the greater because the people
themselves proved his belief wrong. He could not then
blame any individual senator or group of senators for the
defeat of the League; he could not place the onus for its
defeat on the Republican party: the people of America, the
President told Tumulty, "have disgraced us in the eyes of the

world."[27] Ironically Lodge concurred with the opinion that "the people at large were much more decided about not having anything to do with the League of Nations than were the men in public life."[28]

There was much insight in the letter that Senator John Sharp Williams, an ardent advocate of the League, wrote Wilson after his election defeat. "God didn't create the world in one act," wrote Williams. It was scarcely possible, he added, that the campaign for the League of Nations could be won in the first battle. The weight of tradition was too great; the people felt that the "voice of the Fathers" had been in the "opposite direction." "The people can learn though not quickly."[29]

Later Wilson himself agreed with Williams' interpretation of events. Not long before his death he said to the members of his family circle: "It was right that the United States did not join the League of Nations. . . . I've been thinking about this for a long time. If we had joined the League when I asked for it, it would have been a great personal victory. But it would not have worked, because deep down in their hearts the American people didn't really believe in it. The time will come when this country will join such a league because they will know that it has to be. And then and then only will it work."[30]

A government by the people is one in which the mistakes are made by the elected representatives. The Senate defeated the League, it has often been said, as though the Senate were an autonomous clique not chosen by or responsible to the American people. The Senate was intended to be and is conservative and slow to act, but it is responsive and responsible. While it may be dominated for a time by strong personalities representing a minority opinion, and while it traditionally respects the right of any senator, even though he be a minority of one, to express and hold to his opinion, the Senate must over a period of time conform to the public will. Thus it may be assumed that a mere squabble in the Senate over the wording of reservations to Article Ten of the League Covenant could not have long prevented American entry into an organization supported by overwhelming American opinion. The events in the years following the defeat of the League in 1920 underscore time and again the

fundamental objection of the Senate to adopting a foreign
policy involving any such hard and fast commitments and
responsibilities as were outlined in Article Ten. At the same
time the public concurred in this judgment. There was
never enough division of opinion to make internationalism
a profitable campaign issue during the next two decades.

Notes

CHAPTER I

[1]Robert Lansing, *The Peace Negotiations: A Personal Narrative* (Boston, 1920), 303.

[2]Merle Curti, *Peace or War: The American Struggle* (New York, 1936), 28.

[3]William Graham Sumner, "The Fallacy of Territorial Extension," *Forum*, XXI (June, 1896), 418.

[4]Woodrow Wilson, "Democracy and Efficiency," *Atlantic Monthly*, LXXXVII (Feb., 1901), 291.

[5]William Ladd, *An Essay on a Congress of Nations for the Adjustment of International Disputes Without Resort to Arms*, Reprinted from the original edition of 1840 by the Carnegie Endowment (New York, 1916), 75ff.

[6]Harold and Margaret Sprout, *The Rise of American Naval Power, 1776-1918* (Princeton, 1946), 227.

[7]A. C. F. Beales, *The History of Peace* (London, 1931), 262.

[8]*Independent*, LXXXI (Jan. 4, 1915), 4.

[9]*Ibid.*, LXX (May 11, 1911), 995-999; 1021-1023.

[10]*Congressional Record*, 59 Cong., 1 sess., 1730; *Independent*, LXXX (July 20, 1914), 83.

[11]*Ibid.*, 61 Cong., 2 sess., 4020-4021, 4027.

[12]*Ibid.*, 4017, H.R. 125.

[13]*Ibid.*, 7432, H. J. R. 223.

[14]*Ibid.*, 63 Cong., 2 sess., 479-480.

[15]*Ibid.*, 63 Cong., 3 sess., Index 1 - 5, S. J. R. 233; S. J. R. 219; H. J. R. 59; H. J. R. 396.

[16]*Ibid.*, 64 Cong., 1 sess., 8813; Navy Dept., Annual Reports, 1920, 3.

[17]W. Stull Holt, *Treaties Defeated by the Senate* (Baltimore, 1933), 207.

[18]*Ibid.*, 211

[19]William Clinton Olson, "Theodore Roosevelt's Conception of an International League," *World Affairs Quarterly*, XXIX (Jan., 1959), 330.

[20]*Independent*, LXXIX (Jan. 4, 1915), 4.

[21]Olson, "Theodore Roosevelt's Conception of an International League," 338.

[22]*Ibid.*, 340-341.

[23]*Ibid.*, 345-346.

[24]*Ibid.*, 346-348; *Independent*, LXXIX (Jan. 4, 1915), 13-17.

[25]*Ibid.*, 351n; Theodore Roosevelt, *America and the World War*, XX, in the *Works of Theodore Roosevelt*, 24 vols., Hermann Hagedorn, ed. (New York, 1925).

[26]*Independent*, LXX (May 11, 1911), 995-999; LXXIX (Sept. 28, 1914), 427-428.

[27]*Report on the Twenty-first Annual Lake Mohonk Conference on International Arbitration*, May, 1915 (Published by the Conference, 1915), 51-56.

[28]Theodore Marburg, *Development of the League of Nations Idea: Documents and Correspondence of Theodore Marburg*, 2 vols., John H. Latane, ed. (New York, 1932), II, 703-717.

[29]*Independent*, LXXXII (June 14, 1915), 459.

[30]Latane, *Development of the League of Nations Idea*, I, 32, 39-40.

[31]Ruhl J. Bartlett, *The League to Enforce Peace* (Chapel Hill, 1944), 36, 39, 42; *Win the War for Permanent Peace* (Published by the League to Enforce Peace, 1918).

[32]*Independent*, LXXXII (June 28, 1915), 523.

[33]Richard Current, "The United

States and 'Collective Security:' Notes on the History of an Idea," Alexander DeConde, ed. (Durham, N.C., 1957), 35.

[34]Henry F. Pringle, *The Life and Times of William Howard Taft*, 2 vols. (New York, 1939), II, 927-928.

[35]*Ibid.*, 930.

[36]*Independent*, LXXXII (June 14, 1915), 459.

[37]Pringle, *Taft*, II, 930.

[38]*Report on the Twenty-second Annual Lake Mohonk Conference on International Arbitration*, May 1916, 144-147.

[39]John A. Garraty, *Henry Cabot Lodge* (New York, 1953), 344.

[40]Bartlett, *League to Enforce Peace*, 20, 43.

[41]Elting Morison, ed., *The Letters of Theodore Roosevelt*, 8 vols. (Cambridge, 1951), II, 927,928.

[42]*Report on the Twenty-second Annual Lake Mohonk Conference on International Arbitration*, May, 1916, 100-108.

[43]*Ibid.*, 144-146.

[44]Beales, *The History of Peace*, 303.

[45]Henry R. Winkler, *The League of Nations Movement in Great Britain, 1914-1919* (New Brunswick, N. J., 1952), 246-247; Beales, *The History of Peace*, 287.

CHAPTER II

[1]Harley Notter, *The Origins of the Foreign Policy of Woodrow Wilson* (Baltimore, 1937), 43, 331.

[2]*Cong. Rec.*, 64 Cong., 1 sess., App. 2160.

[3]Herbert Hoover, *The Ordeal of Woodrow Wilson* (New York, 1958), 253-261.

[4]Robert Langer, *Seizure of Territory: The Stimson Doctrine and Related Principles in Legal Theory and Diplomatic Practice* (Princeton, 1947), 34-37.

[5]Samuel F. Bemis, "Woodrow Wilson and Latin America," Edward H. Buehrig, ed., *Wilson's Foreign Policy in Perspective* (Bloomington, 1957), 131.

[6]*Cong. Rec.*, 62 Cong., 1 sess., 27-28; 63 Cong., 1 sess., 357.

[7]Notter, *Foreign Policy of Woodrow Wilson*, 273.

[8]Bemis, "Woodrow Wilson and Latin America," 131-132.

[9]Notter, *Foreign Policy of Woodrow Wilson*, 326-328.

[10]E. M. House, *The Intimate Papers of Colonel House*, arranged by Charles Seymour, 6 vols. (Boston, 1926-1928), I, 208-209.

[11]Ray Stannard Baker, *Woodrow Wilson: Life and Letters*, 8 vols. (New York, 1927-1939), VI, 83n.

[12]Notter, *Foreign Policy of Woodrow Wilson*, 358-359.

[13]*Ibid.*, 105.

[14]*Ibid.*, 328-332; Baker, *Wilson*, V, 74.

[15]Seymour, *House*, I, 208-209.

[16]*Ibid.*, 209-210.

[17]Bemis, "Woodrow Wilson and Latin America," 135.

[18]Charles H. Carlisle, "Woodrow Wilson's Pan-American Pact," *Proceedings of the South Carolina Historical Association*, XIX (1949), 3-15.

[19]Seymour, *House*, I, 232; Bemis, "Woodrow Wilson and Latin America," 134-135.

[20]*Ibid.*, 365.

[21]*Ibid.*, 365.

[22]*Independent*, LXXXVI (May 22, 1916), 264-265.

[23]Baker, *Wilson*, VI, 212-213.

[24]Robert Lansing, *Peace Negotiations*, 34.

[25]*Independent*, LXXXVI (May 22, 1916), 264.

[26]*Ibid.*, June 5, 1916, 356-357.

[27]Bartlett, *League to Enforce Peace*, 55.

[28]Notter, *Foreign Policy of Woodrow Wilson*, 541-542.

[29]Edgar E. Robinson and Victor J. West, eds., *The Foreign Policy of Woodrow Wilson* (New York, 1918), 334, 337, 347, 348, 351, 353, 355, 357, 359.

[30]Baker, *Wilson*, VI, 206.

CHAPTER III

[1]Arthur Link, *Wilson the Diplomatist: A Look at His Major Foreign Policies* (Baltimore, 1957), 23.

[2]Baker, *Wilson*, VI, 381.

[3]Dexter Perkins, *Hands Off: A History of the Monroe Doctrine* (Baltimore, 1940), 284-285.

[4]Robinson and West, *Foreign Policy of Wilson*, 359-362.

[5]Claudius O. Johnson, *Borah of Idaho* (New York, 1936), 224.

[6]Baker, *Wilson*, VI, 418.

[7]Robinson and West, *Foreign Policy of Woodrow Wilson*, 362-370.

[8]Notter, *Foreign Policy of Woodrow Wilson*, 604-606.

[9]John Chalmers Vinson, *William E. Borah and the Outlawry of War* (Athens, Ga., 1957), 19.

[10]Henry Cabot Lodge, *The Senate and the League of Nations* (New York, 1925), 281-296.

[11]Edward H. Buehrig, "Woodrow Wilson and Collective Security," Edward H. Buehrig, ed., *Wilson's Foreign Policy in Perspective*, (Bloomington, 1957), 52-53.

[12]*Foreign Relations of the United States, The Lansing Papers, 1914-1920*, 2 vols. (Washington, 1939), I, 20-22.

[13]Robinson and West, *Foreign Policy of Woodrow Wilson*, 387-389.

[14]Current, "Collective Security," 37-38.

[15]*Independent*, LXXXVI (May 22, 1916), 264.

[16]Hoover, *The Ordeal of Woodrow Wilson*, 254.

[17]Link, *Wilson the Diplomatist*, 100-102.

[18]Baker, *Wilson*, VII, 53.

[19]Seymour, *House*, IV, 9.

[20]Pringle, *Taft*, 937, 939.

[21]*Ibid.*, 932-934.

[22]*Ibid.*, 939.

[23]Baker, *Wilson*, VI, 97.

[24]*Ibid.*, VII, 203; Seymour, *House*, IV, 12, 16.

[25]Earl Willis Crecraft, "A League of Nations in the Making," *New York Times*, Dec. 2, 1918.

[26]Seymour, *House*, IV, 49.

[27]*Ibid.*, 38

[28]*Ibid.*, 52. Wiseman to Lord Reading, Aug. 16, 1918. This cablegram was drafted by House.

CHAPTER IV

[1]Bartlett, *League to Enforce Peace*, 99-107.

[2]Robert Lansing, *Confidential Diary*, Library of Congress, Dec. 16, 1918.

[3]Seymour, *House*, IV, 280-282.

[4]Robert Lansing, *Confidential Diary*, *Appendix*, Library of Congress, Dec. 8, 1918.

[5]Lansing, *Confidential Diary*, Sept. 30, Oct. 18, Nov. 12, 1918; *Confidential Diary*, *Appendix*, Dec. 4, 1918.

[6]Lansing, *Confidential Diary*, *Appendix*, Dec. 11, 1918.

[7]Lansing, *Confidential Diary*, Dec. 18, 1918.

[8]*Ibid.*, Dec. 21, 1918.

[9]Albert Beveridge Papers, Library of Congress, Box 211, Beveridge to James M. Beck, Aug. 21, 1919; Box 212, Beveridge to P. C. Knox, Dec. 9, 1918.

[10]Allan Nevins, *Henry White: Thirty Years of American Diplomacy* (New York, 1930), 355.

[11]Beveridge Papers, Box 212, Knox to Beveridge, Dec. 9, 1918.

[12]Denna Frank Fleming. *The United States and the League of Nations* (New York, 1932), 77-80.

[13]Lansing, *Confidential Diary*, Jan. 6, 1919.

[14]*Ibid.*, Jan. 7, 1919.

[15]Senate Document 106, 66 Cong., 1 sess., 1177ff.

[16]Lansing, *Confidential Diary*, Jan. 7, 8, 10, 1919.

[17]*Ibid.*, Jan. 11, 1919.

[18]Lansing, *Peace Negotiations*, 94-95.

[19]Buehrig, "Woodrow Wilson and Collective Security," 57-59.

[20]Lansing, *Peace Negotiations*, 81-92, 295-298.

[21]Seymour, *House*, IV, 306-307, 313, 314-315.

[22]*Ibid.*, 315-317.

[23]Fleming, *The United States and the League of Nations*, 120-121.

[24]Chandler P. Anderson, *Diary*, Box IV, Library of Congress, March 13, 1919.

[25]Seymour, *House*, IV, 385-386.

[26]Fleming, *The United States and the League of Nations*, 140-146.

[27]Anderson, *Diary*, Box IV, March 13, 1919.

[28]Fleming, *The United States and the League of Nations*, 154-156.

[29]Thomas A. Bailey, *Woodrow Wilson and the Lost Peace* (New York, 1944), 206.

[30]*Ibid.*, 202-203.

[31]*Ibid.*, 207-208.

[32]*Ibid.*, 211; Arthur Walworth, *Woodrow Wilson: World Prophet*, 2 vols. (New York, 1958), II, 284.

[33]Seymour, *House*, IV, 340.

[34]*Ibid.*, 373.

[35]Lansing, *Confidential Diary*, March 19, 1919; *Peace Negotiations*, 206-207.

[36]Notter, *Origins of Wilson's Foreign Policy*, 594n.

[37]Seymour, *House*, IV, 351-352.

[38]*Ibid.*, 352-353.

[39]Walworth, *Wilson*, II, 286.

[40]Bailey, *Woodrow Wilson and the Lost Peace*, 211-216.

[41]Perkins, *Hands Off*, 294-298.

[42]Buehrig, "Woodrow Wilson and Collective Security," 54-56.

[43]Walworth, *Wilson*, II, 301.

[44]*Ibid.*, 305.

CHAPTER V

[1]Nevins, *White*, 395-400.

[2]*Root Papers*, Library of Congress, Miscellaneous Papers, 1919.

[3]Anderson, *Diary*, Box VI, March 13, 1919.

[4]*Ibid.*; Nevins, *White*, 400-401. The cable, says Nevins, was kept confidential.

[5]Root Papers, Box 231, Root to Lodge, March 13, 1919; Lodge to Root, March 14, 1919.

[6]*Ibid.*, Stimson to Root, March 19, 1919; Will H. Hays, *Memoirs* (New York, 1955), 202.

[7]Hays, *Memoirs*, 196.

[8]Beveridge Papers, Frank Munsey to Beveridge, April 7, 1919.

[9]Hays, *Memoirs*, 197-202.

[10]Oscar S. Straus, "Mr. Root and Article 10; His Conflicting Views," *New York Times*, June 22, 1919.

[11]Elihu Root, *Miscellaneous Addresses*, Robert Bacon and James Brown Scott, eds. (Cambridge, 1917) 281-294. Address to the American Association of International Law, April 26, 1917.

[12]Root Papers, Box 231, Root to House, August 16, 1918; Root sent a copy to Henry White also, November 30, 1918.

[13]Anderson, *Diary*, Box IV, Dec. 12, 1918.

[14]Root Papers, House to Root, Aug. 23, 1918.

[15]Richard Leopold, *Elihu Root and the Conservative Tradition* (New York, 1954), 123-130.

[16]Anderson, *Diary*, Box IV, March 10, 1919.

[17]Root Papers, Root to John Kendrick Bangs, April 2, 1919.

[18]*Ibid.*, Root to Lawrence Lowell, April 29, 1919.

[19]*Ibid.*, Root to George Barrow, June 28, 1919.

[20]*Ibid.*, Root to John Kendrick Bangs, April 2, 1919.

[21]Leopold, *Root*, 130-134.

[22]Perkins, *Hands Off*, 294.

[23]Thomas A. Bailey, *Woodrow Wilson and the Great Betrayal* (New York, 1944), 14.

[24]Root Papers, Box 231, Lodge to Root, April 29, 1919.

[25]*Ibid.*, Root to Brandegee, June 8, 1919; Brandegee to Root, June 9, 1919.

[26]Hays, *Memoirs*, 203.

[27]*Ibid.*, 203-205; Philip Jessup, *Elihu Root*, 2 vols. (New York, 1938), II, 399-401.

[28]Hays, *Memoirs*, I, 211-212.

[29]Root Papers, Box 231 to Kellogg, Nov. 12, 1919.

[30]*Ibid.*, Root to Lodge, May 14, 1920.

[31]Anderson Papers, *Diary*, Box IV, Dec. 4, 1919.

[32]Root Papers, Box 231, Root to Lodge, July 3, 1919.

[33]*Ibid.*, Root to Lodge, July 24, 1919.

[34]*Ibid.*

[35]*Ibid.*, Root to George Clinton, June 28, 1919.

[36]Charles Evans Hughes Papers, Library of Congress, Box 171, Beerits Memo, League of Nations.

[37]Root Papers, Box 231, Root to Lodge, July 3, 1919.

[38]Hughes Papers, Box 171, Beerits Memo, League of Nations.

[39]William E. Borah Papers, Library of Congress, Box 237, Hughes to Borah, Aug. 2, 1919.

[40]Taft Papers, Library of Congress, Box 84, Taft to Fred Brewster, Feb. 15, 1916; Bartlett, *League to Enforce Peace*, 155.

[41]*Ibid.*, Taft to Casper Vost, May 22, 1919; Bartlett, *League to Enforce Peace*, 155.

[42]*Ibid.*, Taft to Arthur Vandenberg, June 4, 1919.

[43]*Ibid.*, Taft to Frank B. Kellogg, June 10, 1919.

[44]Walworth, *Wilson*, I, 345n.

[45]Bartlett, *League to Enforce Peace*, 142-145; Taft Papers, Taft to Gus Karger, July 10, 1919, July 13, 1919; Taft to Short, July 18, 1919; Taft to Arthur Vandenberg, Sept. 21, 1919; Root Papers, Hays to Root, July 17, 1919; Lodge to Root, July 28, 1919.

[46]Taft Papers, Box 84, Taft to Gus Karger, Feb. 6. 1916.

[47]*Ibid.*, Box 132, Taft to Charles Hilles, Nov. 8, 1919; Taft to Gus Karger, April 24, 1920.

[48]*Ibid.*, Box 131, Taft to Porter J. McCumber, Aug. 26, 1919; Taft to Arthur Vandenberg, September 21, 1919. Taft wrote many times that the Treaty could not be adopted without reservations.

[49]Gilbert Hitchcock Papers, Library of Congress, Taft to Hitchcock, Nov. 19, 1919.

[50]Beveridge Papers, Box 212, Lodge to Beveridge, Nov. 23, 1918; Lodge to Beveridge, December 3, 1918; Garraty, *Lodge*, 345-346.

[51]*Ibid.*, Box 216, Lodge to Beveridge, December 30, 1918.

[52]*Ibid.*, Lodge to Beveridge, Jan. 4, 1919; Jan. 28, 1919; Feb. 18, 1919; Feb. 20, 1919.

[53]*Ibid.*, March 8, 1919; March 21, 1919.

[54]Nevins, *White*, 399.

[55]Beveridge Papers, Box 212, March 8, 1919; March 21, 1919.

[56]Borah Papers, Box 550, Albert Beveridge to Borah, April 27, 1919.

[57]*Ibid.*, Beveridge to Borah, June 16, 1919.

[58]*Ibid.*, Lodge to Beveridge, June 23, 1919.

[59]*Ibid.*, Lodge to Beveridge, Aug. 4, 1919.

[60]Bartlett, *League to Enforce Peace*, 161n.

[61]Root Papers, Lodge to Root, Sept. 3, 1919.

CHAPTER VI

[1]Woodrow Wilson Papers, File VIII, Wilson to Tumulty, May 2, 1919; Apparently Wilson considered running for a third term as a means of assuring acceptance of the League. Wilson to Tumulty, June 2, 1919; Senator Spooner, June 7, invited Wilson to make his first speech on a western tour at St. Louis.

[2]Walworth, *Wilson*, II, p. 341.

[3]*Ibid.*, 343.

[4]Wilson Papers, File VIII, Wilson to House, March 3, 1919; Wilson to John Sharp Williams, January 13, 1919.

[5]Holt, *Treaties Defeated by the Senate*, 207, 234.

[6]Lansing, *Confidential Diary*, May 27, 1919.

[7]Fleming, *The United States and the League of Nations*, 250-252.

[8]*Ibid.*, 149-150.

[9]*Ibid.*, 322-323, 290-291.

[10]*Ibid.*, 277.

[11]*Ibid.*, 279-283.

[12]Walworth, *Wilson,* 343.
[13]Lansing, *Confidential Diary, Appendix,* Aug. 2, 1919; Aug. 11, 1919.
[14]Lodge, *Senate and the League of Nations,* 351-358.
[15]Walworth, *Wilson,* II, 359.
[16]Bailey, *Great Betrayal,* 171-172; 393-394.
[17]*Ibid.,* 393-394.
[18]Walworth, *Wilson,* II, 344.
[19]Hoover, *The Ordeal of Woodrow Wilson,* 254-257.
[20]Walworth, *Wilson,* II, 373.
[21]David F. Houston, *Eight Years in Wilson's Cabinet,* 2 vols. (New York, 1926), 6.
[22]Link, *Wilson the Diplomatist,* 155.

CHAPTER VII

[1]*Foreign Relations, 1917, Supplement,* Vol. I, 24-29.
[2]Link, *Wilson the Diplomatist,* 144.
[3]*Ibid.,* 143; Houston, *Eight Years with Wilson's Cabinet,* II, 24-26.
[4]Fleming, *The United States and the League of Nations,* 346-357.
[5]Link, *Wilson the Diplomatist,* 148.
[6]Houston, *Eight Years with Wilson's Cabinet,* II, 24-26.
[7]Ruhl J. Bartlett, *Record of American Diplomacy* (New York, 1948), 476-480.
[8]Link, *Wilson the Diplomatist,* 145.
[9]*Ibid.,* 149-150.
[10]Root Papers, Box 231, Root to Lodge, Sept. 10, 1919.
[11]*Ibid.,* Lodge to Root, Sept, 29, 1919.
[12]Bartlett, *League to Enforce Peace,* 140 n.
[13]Anderson Papers, *Diary,* IV, Sept. 21, 1919.
[14]*Ibid.*
[15]*Ibid.,* Oct. 2, 1919.
[16]*Ibid.*
[17]Lodge, *Senate and the League of Nations,* 184.
[18]Anderson Papers, *Diary,* IV, Sept. 26, 1919.
[19]Bailey, *Great Betrayal,* 179.
[20]Lodge, *Senate and the League of Nations,* 184.
[21]Bailey, *Great Betrayal,* 159-160.
[22]Lodge, *Senate and the League of Nations,* 185.
[23]Holt, *Treaties Defeated by the United States Senate,* 297.
[24]Hays, *Memoirs,* 213.
[25]Lansing, *Confidential Diary,* Dec. 16. 1919.
[26]Hays, *Memoirs,* 214.
[27]*Ibid.*
[28]Anderson Papers, *Diary,* IV, Dec. 4, 1919.
[29]*Ibid.,* Nov. 21, 1919.
[30]Beveridge Papers, Box 216, Brandegee to Beveridge, Nov. 28, 1919.
[31]Root Papers, Box 231, Root to Lodge, Dec. 1, 1919.
[32]*Ibid.,* Dec. 3, 1919
[33]Beveridge Papers, Box 216, Lodge to Beveridge, Jan. 3, 1920; Garraty, *Lodge,* 384-387.
[34]Lodge, *Senate and the League of Nations,* 194-195; Bailey, *Great Betrayal,* 402; Garraty, *Lodge,* 383.
[35]Bailey, *Great Betrayal,* 230-231.
[36]Walworth, *Wilson,* II, 391; Hitchcock Papers, Mrs. Wilson to Hitchcock, Jan. 26, 1920.
[37]Bailey, *Great Betrayal,* 244-245.

CHAPTER VIII

[1]*Literary Digest,* LXVII (Oct. 23, 1920), 11, 13.
[2]*New York Times,* Oct. 30, 1920.
[3]*Ibid.,* Oct. 31, Nov. 1, 1920.
[4]*Ibid.,* Aug. 28, 1920.
[5]*Ibid.,* Oct. 8, 1920.
[6]*Ibid.,* Oct. 9, 1920.
[7]*Ibid.,* Oct. 29, 1920.
[8]Pringle, *Taft,* II, 948-949.
[9]*Literary Digest,* LXVII (Oct. 23, 1920), 12.
[10]Bartlett, *League to Enforce Peace,* 188-189.
[11]Hays, *Memoirs,* 216-217.
[12]*Ibid.,* 219.
[13]*Ibid.,* 218.
[14]*New York Times,* Oct. 16. 1920.
[15]James Cox, *Journey Through My Years* (New York, 1946), 278.
[16]*Ibid.,* Hays, *Memoirs,* 218-219.
[17]*New York Times,* Oct. 14, 1920; Bartlett, *League to Enforce Peace,* 191-196; Dexter Perkins, *Charles Evans Hughes* (New York, 1956), 81-83.

[18]Leopold, *Root*, 146-150.

[19]*Literary Digest*, LXVII (Oct. 30, 1920), 9, 10.

[20]*New York Times*, Oct. 24, 29, 1920.

[21]*Literary Digest*, LXVII (Oct. 30, 1920), 9.

[22]*Ibid.*, 11.

[23]*New York Times*, Oct. 30, 1920.

[24]*New Republic*, XXIV (Nov. 3, 1920), 225.

[25]*Ibid.*, (Nov. 10, 1920), 254.

[26]Bailey, *Great Betrayal*, 323; *Independent*, CIV (Nov. 13, 1920), 229.

[27]*Literary Digest*, CXVII (Oct. 30, 1920), 9.

[28]*New Republic*, XXIV (Oct. 20, 1920), 179.

[29]*Independent*, CIV (Nov. 13, 1920), 222.

[30]*Literary Digest*, CXVII (Nov. 13, 1920), 13.

[31]*Ibid.*, 14.

[32]*Ibid.*

CHAPTER IX

[1]Denna F. Fleming, *The United States and World Organization* (New York, 1938), 37n.

[2]Borah Papers, Borah to Allen L. Benson, Box 310, Nov. 5, 1920.

[3]Committee on General Information, Washington Conference, National Archives, Special Bulletin, No. 5.

[4]*New York Times*, Dec. 7. 11, 16, 18, 1920.

[5]*Ibid.*, Dec. 11, 1920.

[6]*Ibid.*, Dec. 15, 1920.

[7]*Ibid.*, Dec. 16, 1920.

[8]Nicholas Murray Butler, *Across the Busy Years*, 2 vols. (New York, 1940), I, 393.

[9]Borah Papers, Box 202, Borah to Admiral W. F. Fallam, Jan. 25, 1921.

[10]*New York Times*, Jan. 15, 1920.

[11]*Literary Digest*, CXVIII (March 19, 1921), 14; J. B. Scott, "The Foreign Policy of the United States," *American Journal of International Law*, XV (April, 1921), 233.

[12]Root Papers, Misc. Letters, Hilles to Harding, Aug. 17, 1921.

[13]Anderson Papers, *Diary*, Box V, Hughes to Anderson, Oct. 28, 1921.

[14]*Literary Digest*, CXXI (Oct. 1, 1921), 7; *New York Times*, Oct. 20. 1921.

[15]C. Leonard Hoag, *Preface to Preparedness: The Washington Disarmament Conference* (Washington, 1941), 129.

[16]*New York Times*, Nov. 26, 1921.

[17]*Ibid.*, Nov. 28, 1921; *Literary Digest*, CXXI (Dec. 10, 1921), 5-6.

[18]*Literary Digest*, CXXI (Dec. 10, 1921), 5-6.

[19]American Delegation Papers, National Archives, Box 298, Senator Lodge.

[20]Bartlett, *League to Enforce Peace*, 201.

[21]Hughes Papers, Hughes to Lawrence Lowell, July 20, 1922.

[22]Bartlett, *League to Enforce Peace*, 202-203.

[23]J. Chal Vinson, "Military Force and American Policy," Alex DeConde, ed., *Isolation and Security*, 68.

[24]*Ibid.*

[25]J. Chal Vinson, *The Parchment Peace: The United States Senate and the Washington Conference* (Athens, 1955), 188-189.

[26]*Ibid.*, 192, 214.

[27]Garraty, *Lodge*, 400.

[28]George C. Osborn, *John Sharp Williams* (Baton Rouge, 1943), 265.

[29]Charles Beard, *American Foreign Policy in the Making* (New York, 1944), 19.

BIBLIOGRAPHICAL NOTE

In treating a topic already the subject of extensive research and writing it is necessary, of course, to draw heavily from secondary accounts. This debt is acknowledged in the footnotes. As these notes are relatively brief no separate list of authors and titles is included. However, to facilitate access to any particular item the names of all authors cited are listed in the index.

Among the primary sources used the most valuable were the Chandler Anderson Papers, including his Diaries, the Robert Lansing Diaries, the Elihu Root Papers, the Albert Beveridge Papers, the William E. Borah Papers, the Charles Evans Hughes Papers, the Woodrow Wilson Papers, the Gilbert Hitchcock Papers, and the William Howard Taft Papers. All of these collections are located in the Manuscripts Division of the Library of Congress.

Index

141